I0521996

Journey from Africa to Achieve the American Dream

Emei Ezidinma

GLOBAL
PUBLISHING
SOLUTIONS

Journey from Africa to Achieve the American Dream by
Emei Ezidinma
Published by Global Publishing Solutions, LLC
923 Fieldside Drive
Matteson, Illinois 60443
www.globalpublishingsolutions.com

Cover Design by Rebecacovers

Library of Congress Control Number:
2023909350
International Standard Book Number:
979-8-9853892-4-1
E-book International Standard Book Number:
979-8-9853892-5-8

Printed in the United States of America

TABLE OF CONTENTS

Introduction

To study and live in the United States of America was indelible in my mind when I was in High school. Our biology teacher was an American Peace Corp volunteer. She told us stories about life in the United States and the opportunities to succeed if one worked hard. I was prepared to work hard to experience it. Several African immigrants have endured untold challenges, obstacles, barriers, and hardships to travel to the United States for myriad rationales. Some travel for vacations, family reunions, weddings, graduation ceremonies, medical treatments, to conduct business, or to attend conferences and seminars. On the other hand, the majority travel for the purpose of pursuing higher education, to create a brighter future in their careers, as well as to succeed in life. I came to the United States as an international student, and through dedication and hard work, I have realized most of my dreams.

In this book, readers are provided with a clear understanding of the processes and challenges encountered in the journey to achieve the American dream and beyond. Issues relevant to sustaining the achievement of the dream are discussed with balanced perspectives. Living the American dream is the belief that anyone, regardless of their birthplace, can achieve success in a nation where upward mobility is possible.

Giving back to the United States received attention in terms of showing appreciation for available opportunities to develop our highest potentials. Myriad ways to give back to our communities and render assistance to the needy are discussed. Tribute is paid to thousands of immigrants who bore the hardships to excel and also to assist others in succeeding on their own journeys.

We are grateful to live in a nation where opportunities exist to actualize individual dreams and give back to society to keep the dream alive. Understanding the strategies needed to succeed is a major component of this endeavor. For those planning to migrate to the United States, the information in this book could be helpful in getting organized and ready for the journey.

"The Journey from Africa to Achieve the American Dream" is a testament to the resilience and determination of immigrants seeking a better life. Through my personal experiences and insights, I aim to provide readers with valuable knowledge and inspiration to overcome challenges, seize opportunities, and make their dreams a reality. Join me on this transformative journey, where the pursuit of the American dream becomes a beacon of hope and the path to a brighter future.

Part One
Chapter One

Fulfilling a Burning Desire/ Embarking on a Metamorphous Journey

During my senior year of high school, I began fantasizing about going to the United States to further my education. I was influenced partly by exciting stories from our biology teacher, an American Peace Corps volunteer. Although one of my brothers attended college in New York, I had not mentioned to him my intentions to travel outside Nigeria to go to college.

I had a friend through a pen-pal relationship who got admission to a college in the United States and thought that I was blessed to have a brother already in a position to provide advice and direction. He suggested that I engage my brother in the process rather than seek outside help. I heeded advice and focused on working with my brother to study in the United States, and we succeeded.

Studying in America

Most discussions among my classmates in the final year were centered on life after high school, specifically plans to attend a post-secondary institution. The debate that generated much enthusiasm was about traveling abroad to study. One might ask why so many students were more interested in learning abroad, since there were already many universities and post-secondary higher institutions in our country. The choice to study in the States was based purely on the availability of a vast array of institutions offering business and specialized courses. Getting higher education abroad provided students with well-equipped schools, quality libraries, laboratories with modern equipment, the opportunity to work and earn income.

Furthermore, since I lived in a boarding school, we were allowed to watch television on weekends. The most popular movies were western movies, with fights between American Indians and cowboys. In addition, we had access to American magazines and periodicals such as *Sports Illustrated, Newsweek, Time*, and *Reader's Digest*. Information from such sources triggered the interest to explore educational opportunities outside the country. Discussions about lifestyle abroad were of much interest to the students, and magazine pictures of American students partying and having good times made a great impression on them.

To most senior students, what mattered was gaining admission into higher institutions after graduation. Those who secured admission, regardless of the location, were highly celebrated and respected.

But it was considered an achievement of a lifetime to gain admission to any American university. The yearning to study abroad was heightened as students began to discuss and congratulate those who had secured admission to colleges and universities. Some of my friends, who knew that I had a brother living in New York, considered me lucky because I had some connection in the United States. Likewise, my relatives were interested in my future educational pursuit. They suggested that I write to my brother asking him to send me an application form for admission. Without hesitation, I wrote to my brother, went to

2

the post office, and mailed the letter to ensure that it was collected and delivered.

Advice from a Mentor

Three years before I came to the United States, I met a friend in a grocery store. He was wearing a hat with an American flag, which attracted my attention. I asked him where he bought it, and he revealed that it was from the United States. We introduced ourselves and agreed to meet at a nearby restaurant the next day to talk further.

At that meeting, he revealed that he had spent fourteen years in the United States working and going to school. He studied business administration and came back to establish a business in the shipping and clearing sector. On several occasions that we met, the conversation centered on his experiences regarding the struggles to balance working full-time and taking full-time classes. While he studied, he took care of every financial responsibility for his family back home.

I was curious to know every detail about my friend's experience in the United States because that was the reason I moved to Lagos: to secure a visa to travel. During our conversation, my friend asked me what I did for a living. I told him that I was waiting to finalize my plans to travel to the United States to attend college. But because it would take some time to get everything in place, it might be necessary to get a job. His face lit up, and he asked for my experience and qualifications.

He suggested that we meet at the same place the next day and asked that I bring my credentials with a letter of reference from anyone who had known me during the last five years. I went home, put my papers in order, getting ready for the interview. I asked my cousin to provide me with the letter of reference, which he gladly wrote. When we met the next day, I handed the papers to him. After examining them, he nodded and smiled. He said that he had some questions before he decided on my employment. Had I any working experience in the shipping industry? I said no but added that I would be willing to learn as much as possible from him. He asked if it was possible to reach my cousin. I provided him with my cousin's office number. He said that I should allow him about three days to gather the necessary information on my application before deciding.

After three days, I didn't hear from him; I became concerned, and wondered what might have caused the delay in his decision. I wanted to go to his office to determine if he had decided on my application, but I thought better of this and gave him a few more days. Fortunately, on the fifth day, his secretary called my cousin and informed him that I should come to the office by 8 AM on Monday.

I was in the office promptly at 8 that Monday. His secretary asked me to wait for another fifteen minutes because he was on a phone call. When he was through with the call, I was asked to go into his office. He stated that he had reviewed my application and collected other essential information to decide. He took a pause. The next word I heard from him was "congratulations" as he informed me that I was hired as an Account Associate. I received a handbook laying out the details of the job's responsibilities. I would work with new accounts. As for the training I had requested, he promised to make available time to

4

provide necessary support and ensure that I was comfortable with the job. I was overwhelmed with excitement. Having this job was helpful not only to generate some income, but also to gain working experience.

After being hired, I worked closely with my boss for the next month and gleaned valuable lessons on a professional approach to signing up new accounts. We worked on lead generation, setting appointments to talk to prospective clients, sales presentations, and tactics to close the deal. At the end of the training period, I was on my own, with instructions to contact my boss if I needed any help.

Because my boss knew about my intent to travel outside the country for further studies, he occasionally asked about my progress in that process. He was pleased that I was interested in my job and promised to provide me with any advice or information related to getting acquainted with admission to American Universities.

He talked about challenges and obstacles he had to deal with during his school days and how it took longer him to graduate because of them. He revealed that he had to take up two jobs to financially support himself and his family back home. He admitted that he had a student visa, which meant that he would pay full tuition, which was more expensive than if he had qualified as an in-state student.

As for financial needs to further my education, he was upfront about the tuition cost. He repeatedly stated that I would need lots of money to go to school, plus additional funds for my living expenses. He suggested that I save as much money as possible to complete my undergraduate degree. He helped me by giving me opportunities to work overtime, to save more money. I worked with the company for six months, during which time I stayed in touch with my brother to gain admission. Again, my boss urged me to be consistent in the application process and never give up. He recommended some reputable schools with moderate tuition costs and accommodating study programs for international students. He talked at length about his school football team and his pride of their performance on the field. He was also aware that my brother in New York was trying to help me secure admission. In the end, he expressed his willingness to support and exhort me in my earnest desire to travel to the United States.

The application processes

For the next six months, my brother and I discussed my study options in detail. We talked about the subject I would major in and what school I would attend. We also considered the tuition costs. The idea of `living in a boarding school appealed to me, and I communicated that to my brother. His idea was that it would be less expensive if I lived with him while attending classes, rather than living in the dormitory, which would deeply escalate the cost of my education during the first year. After much contemplation, we decided to focus on getting admission to a school that was located in his city - one that was closer to where he lived, perhaps one that was accessible by bus route, in case I didn't have a ride home.

To complete my application, there was a long list of documents required by the schools to ensure that I had completed my high school education. My brother informed me that the application process would be faster if I made haste and arranged all the required documents. I took his advice, and the papers were ready within one week. Then, I went to the post office and mailed them.

It took almost a month before I got a response from my brother, and because I was anxious to complete the application process, it seemed as if it took forever. I wrote to my brother weekly to probe the application's progress to ensure that they had received my mail. He told me to be patient as he diligently followed up with the process to make sure that the application was successful. He kept to his word, and in less than one month, I was admitted to a college in Denver, Colorado.

Interview at the U.S. Embassy

My initial visit to the United States embassy required an appointment with one of the embassy representatives for an interview. It happened on a Monday morning, and I had to leave very early, about 5 AM, to catch the bus to get in the long line. It worked out accordingly, and I was the twelfth person to be called. I submitted my documents, and after a thorough review by the screening clerk, I was scheduled for the visa appointment on a Friday.

Before the interview date, I was preoccupied with the thought of who the interviewer would turn out to be. Several thoughts crossed my mind. Do I have all the documents needed? How about payment of required tuition and income statements from my sponsor, who would financially support me throughout my academic years in the school? On several occasions, I went through the documents to ensure that nothing was missing. I didn't want to take chances. I wanted to avoid a second interview by having all the needed documents available.

The interview started at 8 AM sharp on Friday morning. When I was next in line to be called for an interview, I started having panic attacks, and all kinds of thoughts started racing through my mind. The more I tried to replace negative thoughts with positive outcomes; the more time ticked faster for my turn. Finally, it crossed my mind to have faith that God will help me through it for good. In the blink of an eye, the security motioned my turn to go in for the interview.

The U.S. embassy representative who would be interviewing me smiled when he opened the door. This gesture melted away the residue of anxiety in me. With a smile, I greeted him and told him that it was nice to see him. He asked me to sit down and immediately began the interview session.

His first question was, "why do you want to travel to the United States to attend college, when you have universities here in your country?" I told him that attending college in the United States would provide an opportunity to study and learn in an environment with students from all over the world, with diverse perspectives and an exchange of academic knowledge. I added that my school of choice had a history of promoting racial diversity with experienced faculty members who encourage cross-cultural learning to enhance collaboration, corporation, and teamwork. He told me that the answer made sense and suggested moving to the next question.

He asked for the list of required documents, and I handed him the file and allowed him time to review them. Finally, he made some calls to verify some of the papers submitted, and after authenticating the documents, he asked that I go and pay for the processing fees for my visa. With jubilation in my heart and a robust smile on my face, I walked briskly to the cashier and made the payment. Deep down in my heart, I was humbled and grateful to God. I was asked to come back later for my visa, which I did.

A review of the document from the American embassy after the interview indicated that the visa would be ready at 11 AM on Wednesday. So, by 10:30 AM, I was there – headed straight to the cashier to find out if the visa was ready. There were about ten people ahead of me, and I waited patiently to be called to receive the visa envelope. Finally, the security guard called my number, I went into the cashier's office and picked up the visa envelope.

The cashier requested I look over the visa to ensure that the names are spelled correctly to avoid delays resulting from problems with personal identification. The advice was well-taken, and fortunately, I found on error with the names and address. Within two hours after I arrival at the embassy, the documents needed to travel to the United States were in my hand. I thanked the clerk for her assistance. It was a dream that materialized. I was grateful to God from the depth of my heart.

If I had wings, I would have preferred to fly to my home to announce the good news: that I was blessed with the opportunity to travel abroad to pursue my education. Unfortunately, the bus ride seemed longer than expected, as if the bus was crawling at a snail's pace--or perhaps my longing to disclose the news made me impatient. Finally, I reached my destination and got off the bus in a hurry. Within minutes, I was knocking at the door. My cousin answered, and the smile on my face gave him a clue that my trip was successful.

"How did it go?" he asked. I responded by silently handing him the envelope and motioning to open it and see what was inside. He saw the visa and screened it. Other family members rushed to the door to look at the visa. The news filled the air with excitement and words of praise to the Lord. Each family member congratulated me and expressed their support for the journey ahead. As the news spread among extended family members, friends, and acquaintances, they stopped by to congratulate me.

My family members and friends organized a farewell party to show support and encouragement. It was organized in secrecy, and I learned about it three days before the event. To my surprise, there was a huge turnout. The party took place on a Saturday. By 5 PM, guests started arriving, and the house was filled with people within an hour. We kept extra chairs outside, but they were quickly occupied too. The highlight of the events included an opening remark by the chairman, two to three minutes speeches from family members, and words of advice from close friends.

The celebration went on for about four hours. Fifteen minutes before the end of the gathering, I thanked my family for the surprise party and continued support. I thanked the guests for coming. The celebrations ended with final remarks from the chairman. One of the elder members from the family said the closing prayers and gave the benediction.

I had a week left to prepare for the trip. After that, it was time to travel back to the village to see my parents and other relatives and say goodbye. Fortunately, a relative had planned a trip home for some business matters, so I asked him to inform my parents that I would visit them.

The breaking of the Kola nut.

Breaking the Kola nut is a traditional rite, representative of sharing communion with guests. In the Igbo land (located in the Eastern part of Nigeria), when there is a gathering to have a meeting, a celebration of happy occasions, discussion of essential projects, marriage ceremonies, and funeral receptions, the host presents the Kola nut or nuts depending on the number of guests. The traditional name of the Kola nut is called Oje. It is about the size of avocado seed. They vary in size depending on the size of the pod, but it's around the size of an avocado seed.

The host offers the kola nut to welcome his guests to let them know that he is happy to see them. Additionally, the breaking of the Kola symbolizes the importance of togetherness, the spirit of sharing – in good times and bad times – a communion of oneness. There is a saying among the Igbos that he who presents kola wishes his guest healthy and long life. The kola nuts are presented to the head of the household by a young male. My father made the opening remark – he thanked God for making the travel to the United States possible. Then, he presented the kola nut to his relative, who handed the plate to the oldest male in the gathering. Then, it was time to pray.

The elderly man thanked God for making the gathering possible and prayed for the gathering's purpose to be achieved successfully. Then, in one accord, everyone chanted "Ka odi 3 – "let it be so," or" amen." Then he handed the kola plate to a young man to split into smaller pieces to ensure that everyone partook in the communion. Next, children aged five years and above were allowed to eat the kola nut. Later, the host served the food and carefully attended to everyone. Finally, some elders called me aside to pass along their words of wisdom. In about four hours, the gathering ended, and people went home.

Going back to the village where I was born brought back memories of my childhood days. Various landmarks – the playground, where children played with fine sand, dancing squares where great performances took place – looked the same. The first two-story buildings built by two of the richest men in the village looked more diminutive in size, but still intact and standing firm because they were constructed primarily with boulders. Even though borehole wells were ubiquitous, I went to look at the stream where we collected spring water for cooking and drinking. I drank some with a cup, and it tasted as pure as ever.

On my way back from the stream, I took pictures of our church as a reminder of my Christian upbringing. My dad told me how hard they worked to build the church with boulders of different sizes, concrete, and sand. The men focused on bringing in the rocks while women were responsible for supplying water to mix concrete with sand. There were modern buildings all over the village with boreholes and electricity. Several retail stores were built by the marketplace, flanked with three restaurants.

About a quarter of a mile east of the market was a store which sold construction materials – concrete, iron rods, shovels, name them. It was evident that economic development had started. I utilized my last day in the village to have conversations with my parents and other family members. During the sendoff party, I was showered with myriad gifts such as food, clothing, arts, and crafts. Some of the presents were for me to bring to my brother in New York. Among the gifts I took to him were African clothes, roasted cashew nuts, peanuts, and fried plantains. The fried plantain was air-dried to eliminate the oil content and keep it fresh. Since I had to leave in the morning the next day, my dad insisted that my luggage be completely ready before I went to bed, to ensure that nothing was missing for my trip.

It was pretty emotional when I had to say my final goodbye. In his usual way of lifting his children's spirit, my dad held my hands, lifted them, and said, "Son, you will go to America and come home safely. You will not stumble, nor will you go astray; it's not your upbringing. Keep your focus, and you will achieve your dream. Don't forget your culture and homeland. Have love in your heart, and you will receive a lot of love from other human beings all over the world. I hand you over to *Chukwu di na igwe* (the protection of Almighty God who is in heaven)."

I knew that it would not be easy to say goodbye to my mother. I have always been very close to her, and we get along very well. As the last born out of seven children, I received a lot of her time. When my older siblings left the house to live independently, we had the house to ourselves. For her, it was unbearable to think that I was traveling to a foreign land, and that it could take years before I finish my education and come back.

She asked me repeatedly, "When will you come back to see me?" I tried to assure her that I would be back as soon as possible. Before I could add another word of assurance to her questions, she burst into tears, and I held her hand as the tears kept streaming down her cheeks. I had to be strong for her. I kept my composure. I held her tight, looked her in the eye, and told her that I loved her. With those words of comfort and assurance, she calmed down but still breathed hard. She turned and faced me. She asked for my hand. Just as my father did, she held my hands and asked God to be my guide and protector. She prayed that I put God first in all my endeavors and God would take care of all my needs. She finally said, "Whatever you do, reach out to those in need, no matter their ethnicity or culture." I hugged her and told her that I would be back to see her, and she nodded in agreement. My ride was waiting, and we said goodbye to each other, and the car drove off from the family compound.

At the outskirts of the village, there was a landmark that reminded me of my early school days. Although the sign bearing the school's name – UMUOBILA CENTRAL SCHOOL – had been changed several times due to erosion from rain, the name remained the same. My friend asked me if I would like to take pictures of the school for my collection, and I said yes. We got out of the car, to get closer to the building for a bigger and better shot. It was a bright day, and the sky was clear; the pictures were perfect. That was the last stop, and in less than five minutes, we were on our way to the city.

I had three days before my departure when I got back from the village. I made a list of things that needed to be done in order of priority. The first was to ensure that my traveling documents were in order, followed by financial arrangements to cover my educational expenses. After that, I made time to see a few friends who could not come to the sendoff party to say goodbye. I had booked my flight with Lufthansa through an agent before traveling to the village. Two days before departure, I went and collected the travel ticket.

Our plane was scheduled to depart from what was then called Lagos International Airport. I arrived at check-in early two hours earlier, enough time to clear customs. I had some conversations with my relatives who had come to see me off at the airport. Time went by swiftly; I looked at my watch and realized that boarding time was only fifteen minutes away. I picked up my hand luggage and headed to the boarding door. We went through the customs for the final check. The entrance of the plane closed at 12:45 AM, and we departed. I promised myself that this was the beginning of the journey to pursue the American dream. We stopped in Germany to refuel and pick up passengers traveling to the United States. Overlay in Germany was about five hours. By 6 AM, we boarded the plane to New York.

Chapter Two

The New Lifestyle

We landed at John F Kennedy Airport in New York at 4 PM from Germany, and I had to transfer to a local flight to Denver, Colorado. I arrived at the gate on time and had time for a quick lunch before boarding the plane for my next destination. I used the public telephone to inform my brother that we were in New York and about to depart for Denver. He said he was ready to get to the airport in the next three and a half hours to pick me up. I provided him with the airline's name, the flight number, and the arrival time. He promised to be there on time.

It was summer in Denver, and by 8 PM, it was still daylight. The sky was blue, and looking through the plane window, I saw the beautiful Colorado mountains covered with pine trees. Our plane was on time, landing three and a half hours later, as scheduled. I claimed my luggage and headed to the passenger pickup area. Traffic was moderate, and as I looked at the waiting vehicle on the Northside, I saw my brother waving his hand frantically in the air. My heart was filled with immense joy. I knew deep down in my heart: I had arrived. All the stress and anxiety that accumulated in me over this trip disappeared. My brother motioned me to stay where I was as he was waiting for the traffic to clear.

It did not take long before he drove to where I was standing. He got out of the car with a beaming smile. He called my name and told me that I was welcomed – that he was happy I made it to the United States to pursue higher education. We kept the conversation brief- and quickly loaded the luggage in the car and drove off. As we drove home, he asked about our family members. In my response, I succinctly focused on their health, what they were doing or planning to do, and developments such as graduations and marriages. The ride from the airport took about forty-five minutes, so we decided to suspend the conversation – to be continued later.

My brother's family was equally anxious about my arrival. As we drove closer to the house, I could see the window blind primed open. The kids were excited to see their uncle. Their parents had talked about a relative coming to live with them for a while. I gleaned further that the kids were keen on knowing how soon I was coming, the room I would stay in, and what type of African food I was bringing with me. As soon as they spotted the car turning the corner to the house, the garage door rolled up. We pulled into the driveway, got out of the car, and the kids rushed to greet me with their mother. We hugged and talked briefly and continued unloading the luggage into the house. The garage door was closed, and everyone was inside.

The kids jumped on my lap and asked for my name. Before I could respond, their mother interjected and said to them, "Call him uncle." They wanted more time to talk, but I had to take a bath and change my clothes. As dinner was being served, we continued with the conversation about our homeland Nigeria. Finally, it was getting late, and the kids had to go to bed. My brother worked the morning shift, so he got up to go to bed and we said good night to each. I went to my room and closed the door.

17

Although my brother and his family tried to make me feel at home, yet it was not easy to get comfortable with no friends or associates with similar cultural background. It took considerable amount of time to establish meaningful relationships, which reduce boredom and isolation. This section provides insight into significant challenges some immigrants encounter during the early stages of arrival to start a new life in the United States.

I was fortunate to have accommodation with a family member who was willing to assist with food and shelter until I could stand on my feet. However, the struggle with accommodation could get out of hand. There are cases that could result in homelessness, living in a halfway house, or living with families who have extra room to spare.

One of the surprises I experienced was related to differences in daily styles between Nigeria and the United States: attitudes towards work, education, social life, and financial matters. For example, I observed how my brother had to get up early in the morning, come home late, stayed awake to study till late, and still had to go to work the next day. On the other hand, his wife worked equally hard, went to school, and cared for the children. I wondered whether what I observed was real or whether my brother and his wife chose to live in such a manner. One week went by, and the routine was repeated day after day except for Saturdays and Sundays when they were off from work.

After attending church service on a Sunday, we stopped at a restaurant and ordered some food for lunch. It was ordered through the drive-through window, and we had to eat in the car while my brother drove. By the time we got to the house, everybody had finished their food except for drinks. It was close to the end of the semester, and my brother had to prepare for exams.

He had his priorities in order. Every minute of his time was precious. He rushed into his study and had to get his assignment completed before bedtime. The kids went to their rooms to allow him time to study; his wife went to the basement to study equally. I went to my room to write letters to family members to inform them that I arrived safely and in the process of adjusting to the new life style.

Getting Started

The time for registration to start my studies was one week away, and I had to get ready for class. With the help of my brother, we drove to the campus and met the officer responsible for international students' enrollment. He pulled up my file and confirmed my identity. I registered as a full-time student and was asked to proceed to the adjacent room to make payment to the cashier. As the payment was made, I realized that I was at the threshold of a life-changing experience. Being a full-time student meant that I would take at least six to eight classes. It would require undivided attention and constant time management. It was a wake-up call. My priorities obviously needed profound alignment with my class schedule.

I couldn't wait to get in the car to express my concerns to my brother. My brother was a full-time student and worked full-time. I asked him how he juggled being a full-time student and working full time. His response fell short of the answer I had anticipated. Instead, he called my name and said, "We need to sit down and talk about what it takes to succeed in this country. Our folks back home don't get it. They think that dollars grow on trees or slither on the streets, and people simply pick them up and spend them. We shall talk."

I agreed, and we drove home in silence. He unlocked the door and went inside, and I followed. He said that he would like to sit down and talk to me about his experience living in the United States and offer some advice before my classes start on Monday. We agreed to talk on Sunday afternoon after church service was over. To avoid disruption during the meeting, he suggested that we stay in the basement, in my room. I was apprehensive about the details of the conversation – what challenges and expectations he would divulge concerning my education.

From the period we initiated the application process for admission, my brother had inquired if I would be ready to take up the challenges emanating from daily issues to survive and succeed? Now, I didn't have a clear answer because I was unsure where he was going with such questions. However, this time his reasons for asking the question became more vivid.

When it was time to talk, he came to the basement. The television was on. I was watching a football game and heard his footsteps. He told me to turn off the television and come into my room. We needed privacy, and he preferred to close the door to keep the kids from interrupting us.

Facing the Truth

He sat down. He cleared his throat and called my name. He said that I should listen very well. He looked me in the eye and said that I needed to let go of the idea that life is easy in the United States, as perpetuated by those looking from the outside. The glamorous pictures you see in the magazines and movies of high rollers – smoking cigars and kissing beautiful women – are made to entertain you. As a matter of fact, nobody will give you anything of value unless you work for it. There is a misconception I want you to eradicate in your mind, he continued. Throw away the notion of easy living in this country and replace it with the concept of work ethic. I asked him to explain to me what he meant by work ethic.

He posited that work ethic morphed from the belief of early American puritan settlers that good things come from hard work. He maintained that work ethic manifests in one's disposition to duty.

Getting back to the main issue, he said that the preambles of his speech were intended to highlight the importance of hard work in my studies. He talked about putting in long hours of study time to complete assignments and prepare for the next class. He warned me about procrastination and talked about how he was negatively impacted after putting aside study projects until the deadline, which resulted in a poor grade. It was a significant learning experience for him, and he never allowed that to happen to him again. Having talked to me about getting serious with my schoolwork and managing my time effectively, he said that the next issue on his mind was for me to find a job in addition to schoolwork.

It was hard to digest because I had registered for full-time studies, and now I had to get a job to add to the burden. Reluctantly, I nodded my head in agreement and told him to continue. Having a job is necessary to meet financial obligations, he stated. He talked about societal perception of work as a means of achieving social status, economic empowerment, acquiring wealth, and a channel to escape poverty. He reminded me of our father's attitude towards work. Our father believed that the worst mistake for a man is to depend on someone else to achieve financial success, rather than self-efforts which comes through hard work, he said. The more he pointed out to me why it was pertinent to understand the role of hard work in my studies, the more it made sense.

Here is the background which leads to the emphasis on hard work. We came from a country where it was not the norm to have a full-time job and carry a full-time load in school. It was not uncommon to find out that either you focus on your job or put work aside and go to school full-time. The idea of keeping a job and working full time was not the norm of in our society during that time. It was especially unbelievable to think of juggling work and studies simultaneously at the undergraduate level.

By the time I came to start my studies, my brother had lived in the United States for four years. Although we didn't talk about his daily activities, I assumed he went to school, period. To think that he would be studying at the university level and keeping a full-time job seemed ridiculous to me. Finally, I asked him why he never mentioned mixing work and studying, and he said that it was the way of life in this country - that it was not a big deal.

The meeting was not over yet. He said it was necessary to address another issue that impacts progress and success. He stated that accomplishing personal goals and objectives required discipline in this fast-paced society. He delved into the rationale for incorporating self-discipline into strategies for getting through undergraduate studies while working a job that may require standing up for six to eight hours daily for five days. Finally, he gave me some pointers.

1. Keep your focus; don't get distracted easily.
2. Do not procrastinate. Do your job to the best of your ability.
3. Complete your assignments before deadlines, no excuses.
4. Put aside much socializing and manage your time prudently.
5. Don't be late at your job and submit your class projects on time to avoid tardiness and penalty.
6. Don't ever think of dropping out of school for any reason; keep going until your complete the courses and graduate.

He said that it would be possible to attain my goals with successful outcomes with these guidelines. The meeting was over. The next day was Monday, and classes started at 9 AM. I was a full-time student during the first month and I focused on my studies. The idea was to get acclimated to study demands, start well, and then get a job. Fortunately, it worked out because I had established my study routine and had a grip on time management by the end of the semester.

My first job was with a restaurant located in Denver, Colorado. During my job search, I took into consideration my current situation. It was imperative to find a job that would allow me the flexibility to work and go to school full-time. At the interview, I was asked about my current job, past job experiences, and why I wanted to work for the company. I answered that going to school was of high priority to me, and finding a job that would allow for evening classes would be ideal. In terms of work experience, I was not a novice. One of my brothers operated a successful restaurant, and during summer vacations from school, I helped out during peak hours. I was hired and asked to start by the weekend.

Chapter Three

The Academic Experience

Attending higher institutions in the United States was a rewarding experience, leading to job opportunities and personal development, along with socioeconomic contacts. The university has become a multicultural gathering place, where students from all over the world acquire their education with American cultural influence. Taking eight classes, coupled with working full time, was tough to handle, but it was rewarding in that it created an opportunity to put my learning into practices. For many foreign students, work environments become a source of learning to improve their English proficiency and communicate better. In other words, one must have the ability to communicate effectively and to understand what others are saying to establish better relationships for success.

During my first year in school, I met students from different countries who were having problems with English communication. The barrier in communication is prevalent when there is a difference in the language among people from different parts of the world. Grammar and spelling could become a barrier in written communication.

Effective ways to deal with communication problem

Globally, North American Universities possess state-of-the-art facilities such as fully equipped libraries, spacious and well-ventilated classrooms, labs, and sports amenities for international students. Eventually, these universities, which turn into a hub, nurture students to have big dreams, build successful careers, serve their countries, or perhaps participate in and contribute to America's greatness.

One of the research studies by Devon Haynie (2014) revealed that the international student population reached a record-breaking number (886,052) in 2000. This number comprised of undergraduates and graduate students in colleges and universities throughout the country. There was a 25% increase in the number of students as compared to previous years. The composition of this phenomenal growth comprises of students from around the world with China with having the highest number (31%), and the rest belong to Saudi Arabia, Asia, Africa, Europe, and Australia (Haynie, 2014). The purpose of the study was to highlight the language difficulty faced by international students and how to encounter and identify probable solutions.

Although international students are required to acquire English skills to gain admission into American colleges and universities, they must demonstrate their skills through the test of English as a second language (TOFEL). Even if they pass the test, most students still struggle to communicate both orally and in written tasks.

The communication issue can be viewed from different perspectives. Some students learn to speak English but may have an accent which makes it difficult to understand what they say. I met students from francophone countries who barely speak English. For them, communication becomes problematic to the extent that gaining admission to schools and finding decent jobs are elusive tasks.

Part of the communication problem stems from pronunciation. Most international students admit that the pronunciation of English words caused breakdowns in communication. In a study conducted by KUO (2011) to elucidate problems international students encounter with the English language, 152 students were interviewed. Many types of communication problems were reported both inside the classroom and outside. Several students said that they had problems with professors and American students because they spoke too fast, especially those with southern accents. On the other hand, American students didn't understand international students because of their heavy accents, and in most cases, they don't have the patience to talk to them.

To deal with communication challenges, international students develop communication strategies to enhance interaction, when there is a breakdown in the process. One of the strategies to avoid communication breakdown is to ask the speaker to repeat what they said. International students are encouraged to open up to people, go out and talk to others and stop being shy. As Kuo stated, "don't be afraid to make mistakes, because we learn through our mistakes and get better." Another strategy is to be interested in the new language, watch the television, and listen to how the words are pronounced (Ku, 2011).

Impacts of Communication Barrier

Dr. Claude was a medical doctor before he won the lottery to come to the United States to practice medicine. Most of his family members are in the medical field. His father was a doctor and his mother a nurse. His twin brother although dead from some form of the disease was a practicing doctor. He entered the country legally with all the legal documents but was unable to practice medicine due to poor communication in English. He is from a Francophone country where the official language is French.

Due to poor communication in English, he can't find a job as a doctor because he has a problem speaking English with clarity. His best bet is to go back to school and learn to write and speak English, He has a menial job with a minimum wage salary. He has been at the same job for over four years with little increase in his hourly rate.

Another example is the case of Sophia who was a nurse before coming to the United States. She had to start as CNA due to communication problem. She started by taking English as a second language and had to get a GED to keep her job. An interview with her revealed that without communication problems, she could easily become the DEO of the nursing home where she worked.

The school environment was an opportunity to understand other challenges immigrants had to endure. Finding a decent job for most African professionals is an issue that many had to endure. There are cases where professionals such as engineers, lawyers, and doctors could not find employment at their level. Most ended up taking menial jobs to survive and remain in such low-skill jobs for years.

On the other hand. there are encouraging stories from immigrants who have experienced hardship in different forms and succeeded in their professions. What impressed me about these professionals who refused to remain at low-level positions was how they went through years of retraining and further studies to become accepted as professionals in their fields.

To overcome the barrier mentioned above, most immigrants discussed how people they knew dealt with communication barriers. One approach was to take classes designed to help those students with English as a second language. Such classes were offered by community colleges or through private tutoring. Other methods included watching television and listening actively to understand how the words are preannounced, as well as how the words sound. It was a matter of paying attention to know how the words are put together. In addition, one has got to put a lot of effort to practice, which in turn allows for improvements to be made over the years.

The ability to speak and communicate effectively cannot be taken for granted to pursue the American dream. There are many benefits derived from effective communication. Clear communication fosters trust with others as well as creates a better understanding of the content of the conversation. It could be embarrassing when one is not understood. Often, we hear questions such as "What did you say?" "Could you repeat what you just said?" "Do you mean to say...?'

Clear communication improves relationships, creates a sense of trust, and reduces misunderstanding. The ability to communicate increases the confidence level of the speaker which is necessary to establish impressive validation of the speech. Equally, clear communication can play a pertinent role in nurturing work experience with a positive rewarding outcome.

To succeed one has to relate to others impressively. Based on information from some immigrants I talked to, many professionals missed the opportunity to excel in their fields mainly because they could not communicate clearly to demonstrate they are experts in their field.

Dealing with societal issues

The challenge to overcome the problems inherent in the language barrier and clear communication is pivotal to integrating into the American culture as well as to achieve the American dream. In the effort to participate and succeed in society it is necessary to examine some issues that exist in the society which people have to deal with. In this section, I focus on issues confronted in the journey to success.

Diversity and Race

Just as the student body is made of up different races, the same applies to society. Unlike the population where I was born, the United States is a melting pot. Although the society in Africa is made of various ethnic groups, the skin color is the same, as is the culture. My idea of American society was far from what I had imagined in terms of how individuals are treated because of their skin color. The longer I lived in the society, the more I realized the racial divide and the way some people become uncomfortable when around those from different racial backgrounds. In my wildest imagination, I couldn't fathom that some people are classified as "people of color."

From an early age, my parents taught me that all human beings are the same created in the image of God. We learned from history and geography about different races living in various areas on our planet. By the time I was in high school, we had access to newspapers and magazines from various parts of the world which displayed pictures of cities and the people living in them. I observed that though we are human beings, there were differences in body tone, and body structures depending on geographical zones around the globe. This is what I call variety in human species, just as we have variety in plants and animals.

For several years, I lived and worked in the city of Lagos, the former capital of Nigeria, with a population of approximately 15 million people. Lagos is considered a metropolitan city. In terms of the population mix, 75% are Nigerians. The original occupants of the land constitute 5 million and the rest are Nigerians from different ethnic tribes.

About 25% of the population are expatriates, as they are called. These are foreigners who came from European countries. Immigrants from African countries amount to 15%, and 10% of the population is made up of Asians, Middle East, and white Europeans and Americans. Among the white population, the British and Americans are higher in number. The current population in 2021 was estimated to reach 20 million people. The color of one's skin is not an issue. What matters is understanding individual uniqueness and respecting people for inalienable human dignity.

Living in Lagos was an opportunity to come in contact with fellow human beings from other parts of the world who now reside in Nigeria. I interacted with them and listened to their stories, why they chose to immigrate and live in Nigeria, their occupation and how long they intend to stay in the country. A good number of immigrants tend to live in the country for the rest of their lives. To them, it is home to them and their families.

For all the years I lived in Nigeria, incidents of discrimination and racial conflicts with foreigners were rare. We lived in the Southwest side of Lagos called Surulere, and in our neighborhood, we have neighbors who migrated from Ghana, Serra Lone, Cameron, United States - both whites and African American. Everyone got along and felt comfortable with each other. That anyone is treated differently based on national origin, skin color, or language was not a familiar experience.

Racial Issues

In this section of the book, I reflected on incidents or close encounters with racial issues which were uncomfortable for me. I made a mental note to explore the experience. Here is the opportunity to address my concern. I spent time researching the fundamental issues which are the root causes of racism even after laws and policies have been enacted against it.

My interest in this matter is anchored on actual experiences with people from different ethnic and racial backgrounds who demonstrated a high degree of acceptance, love, and respect for me as a human being regardless of natural origin, color, or religion. It is a privilege to share years of personal findings regarding racial integration and living in harmony with our neighbors, allowing one another to pursue the American dream uninterrupted.

In addition, these stereotypes and related incidents are discussed to acknowledge their existence and to provide insights on how they could be managed to enhance racial harmony and create a friendlier society. Based on years of dealing with racial and discriminatory practices, adopting the right approach often leads to reconciliatory and more peaceful co-existence.

Stereotype about Africa

Years of stereotypical portrayal of Africa in a negative connotation around the world have created an unhealthy impression of Africans including those in the diaspora, as well as African Americans. The images and pictures coming from Africa are mostly diluted because they are focused more on pictures depicting poverty, hunger, malnutrition, famine, jungle, people living in a primitive environment, and lack of economic development.

I have heard questions about Africa that indicate lack of understanding about both Africa of the past and modern Africa. Due to the unavailability of a balanced review of living standards in Africa, it becomes difficult to understand current trends in the country. On many occasions, I had to explain to non-African friends that Africa is on the move -- developing, growing, and catching up in technology. The goal here is to provide current information in terms of efforts made by Africans through intellectual contribution to economic development, and innovation in the technology and entertainment industry.

Myths About Africa

Before I came to the United States, I had a different world view about human beings, irrespective of their nationality, color, or status. In other words, we are all humans with various cultural differences. However, from observation, I realized that people of African descent were treated with less respect compared to people of other nationalities. For example, I have been asked how I came to the United States. Other times someone wants to know what type of houses we live in or if we have cars on the streets. In addition, the type of news coverage about Africa is often negative.

To most people, Africans are still considered very much undeveloped, and this notion cast African people in the United States as less knowledgeable compared with the rest of the society. The fact of the matter is that the negative mental picture people have about Africa is erroneous, because most African countries are pulling their weights.

In the year 1992, I incorporated a nonprofit organization called African Awareness Expos Inc. The organization was dedicated to promoting African culture and disseminating positive African cultural values, as well as espousing Africa's contribution to civilization. We offered cultural programs to schools, organizations, and government agencies. The purpose of running such an organization was to give back to society and help America understand Africa and its people in a more positive stance.

Here are common questions about Africa and the responses to them.

What do you say about poverty in Africa?

There are poor people in every country in the world; even in the richest countries in the world, there are people who go to bed without any food. The point is that most of the pictures coming out of Africa are negative in content. They depict horrible and demoralizing conditions to cast a more negative image of Africa. Millions of Africans live comfortably and in healthy conditions, but they are hardly shown on television. According to Global Citizen (2018), one out of three Africans is defined as middle class and the number continues to increase. While most Western economies are struggling, African economies continue to grow. A report by Global citizen indicates that six out of the ten fastest economies in the world are in Africa.

Is Africa a jungle as portrayed in the movies and magazines?

The portrayal of Africa as a backward and primitive continent is erroneous and lacks a candid depiction of Africa. Most of the capitals of African countries could be described as modernized and developing at impressive rates **(Please see the pictures of African modern cities at www.google.com (search for African modern cities)).**

Is it true that Africans don't like African Americans?

That is an assertion without validity. We have the same ancestry and heritage, so that is not the case. It is important to understand, as I mentioned earlier, that human beings are the same. Treat them with love and respect and you get along. I went on to expatiate on the answer. For example, the person who asked me this question later became my friend. It didn't happen overnight, but with years of getting to know each other better. We realized that we have a lot in common and enjoyed the company of each other.

People who are friendly and understand the value of being nice often get along with one another regardless of their nationality or gender. On the other hand, some people are hard to get along with, perhaps as a result of bad experiences in life, which may influence their behavior to react negatively. In addition, when people are biased against others based on what they are told, that could also affect their behavior when in contact with others who don't look like them.

How do you feel about racism in America?

To be frank about it, it was a big surprise to notice that so much emphasis was placed on skin color. It was Dr. Rev. Martin Luther King who summed it up the best. His words about racism resonate with me. He said that people should not be judged by the color of their skin but rather by the content of their character.

I was born and raised in a country where the color of somebody's skin was not an issue. It may sound strange, but it is true. In Nigeria, we have people whose skins are white. From their hair to the rest of their body is white. We see such variance as normal, nothing more than a variety of life. Realistically, what matters most is the understanding of our differences which are rooted in cultural or regional locations. People are shaped as a result of their environment, tradition, customs, and what is important to them to make meaning of existence.

On the other hand, I think that we have come a long way in bridging the gap on racism. Society as a whole has come to recognize that racism is real. People are willing to talk about it. It is discussed on social media, articles, books, and many authors have written about it. It is discussed on talk shows and in the classrooms. The government, from federal to local levels, has enacted laws to eradicate racism because it is destructive behavior, which if unchecked could lead to mistreatment of a certain group within the society.

I think that we are making progress in terms of racial harmony, as people begin to recognize our commonalities rather than our differences. Even in corporate environments, management is pushing for better racial integration through the encouragement of diversity programs. Sensitivity programs are encouraged to transform the work environment to become more accommodative for people of all races.

We must not forget men and women who have fought for equality, civil rights, and racial justice. The purpose of engaging in various civil activities is to speak out against injustice and disrespect for some ethnic groups. We must learn to co-exist in peace - leverage our commonalities to grow and overcome any remnants of racism in our society.

Do you have African Americans who live in Africa and how are they treated?

The answer to the question is a resounding yes. I can't quantify the number of African Americans living in Africa or the number living in any particular African country. One thing I know for sure is that when I lived in Lagos Nigeria, three African American families lived on our street. When I was in the African clothing business, I knew of some African Americans who moved back to Ghana to start import and export businesses.

In terms of how African Americans are treated, the African continent traditionally has a culture that is rooted in elaborate - hospitality. Extra care is taken to ensure that visitors from other countries are given attention, treated with respect, and accorded assistance to feel comfortable. Everyone regardless of the color of their skin or nationality is accepted and treated with dignity. In sum, people move freely and mix up easily without focusing on nationality or race.

Without a doubt, it is imperative to address the issue of racial discrimination to figure out how to get around it. There is a conundrum in human relations that if it is ignored would impede progress and stunt personal growth and success. The first step in my analysis is to recognize that racism and prejudice exist and are perpetuated by myth, fear, subjective opinions, bad experience, and unfounded beliefs.

In my review, dealing with racism and discrimination begins with understanding why people embrace and perpetuate racism. As humans, it is easy to copy behaviors and perhaps maintain that our actions are correct because nobody challenges them. Until we recognize that our negative attitude towards others could be offensive, destructive, and repulsive, our behaviors will remain unchanged. What I found out works for me is to be truthful in our attitude and behavior towards others. The number one approach is to get rid of prejudgment of people, because in most cases what we think and believe becomes our reality.

Be realistic. Tell the truth to yourself and the truth will set you free. Naturally, people are good; they are made to be peaceful, loving, and kind. Forget about the color of the skin, or if the person is a man or a woman. Everyone wants to be recognized as a being – to be respected, period. Once you set out with these thought patterns the rest is history. Give love and respect and it will come back to you.

The following tips helped turn negative situations into positive mood with successful outcomes.

1. Don't get offended when you notice behaviors or statements that are not appropriate. Keep your cool, look the person in the eye, and with a smile ask how he or she is doing. Get to business.

2. Don't put yourself in a bind by being afraid or intimidated when talking to someone regardless of their color. Be respectful, friendly, and polite. People are good and ready to help. I have experienced it.

3. Your attitude matters. Present yourself with confidence, which is necessary to create a good impression.

4. You are human first. Don't be preoccupied with the color of your skin. Your attitude determines to a great extent the reception you receive.

5. Appearance is critical to success. There is an African proverb that comes to mind in terms of appearance. It says: You eat with your eyes first. In other words, appearance plays a pertinent role in terms of how the other person perceives you. If the impression is positive,

acceptance and respect are likely to follow and if the impression is negative it could result in a lack of respect and acceptance.

6. Avoid talking too fast to ensure effective communication with the listener.

7. End every conversation with "thank you." It costs nothing to smile, but the reward is more than money can buy.

Overreacting to every discriminatory or racial incident could close the door to opportunities, put a barrier to building productive relationships, impede business networking and limit mental and spiritual growth. Bear in mind that deep inside, we as humans have more commonalities than differences. A negative attitude is low-energy and can be reversed by a positive attitude. To second-guess why the other person is reacting with poor behavior may not yield a rewarding dividend. It's always helpful to understand that people may adopt defensive mechanisms during a first-time encounter. It should not be misinterpreted as unfriendly behavior. A little smile and a light joke can make the encounter a more positive one.

Fear, on the other hand, could lead to an unproductive encounter. Dispel fear with a warm greeting, bold handshake, and remind your guest that it feels good to meet him or her. This type of feeling could trigger a warm feeling between both of you. Recollecting negative incidents may not be the right approach. Instead, utilize what works: Creating positive outcomes through a positive attitude such as a friendly smile, clear communication, and getting to the point.

It is often said that the truth shall set you free. The basic fact is that human beings regardless of size, gender, looks, nationality, intelligence, wealth, or color of the skin possess common human traits. All human souls yearn to be respected, loved, and to live in peace and harmony. We like to succeed and take care of ourselves as well as those who depend on us. Knowing these facts, which are inherent in our genetic make-up, is enough rationale to treat each other with kindness and acceptance.

Clear communication has lots of benefits. The listener has an easier time understanding what is being said, and that allows for an accurate response. More information can be exchanged when the communication is patently structured, which can swing doors wide open for opportunities. It is difficult to engage in an interaction where the exchange of information is replete with misunderstanding.

It is of critical importance for people to know they are appreciated for talking with us, sharing information, and engaging in business activities. Don't forget the most common phrase of appreciation in any interaction. To say "thank you" at the end of the interaction is the most powerful demonstration of respect for people's time and attention in any encounter. Saying "thank you" is rewarding, easy, and results in instant gratification.

Pursuing the American dream is encapsulated in the quest for knowledge from years of investment in-class work, team projects, conducting experiments, writing articles, and completing research studies on various disciplines. Further, knowledge is a derivate of an analytical approach to reviewing other authors' works, refuting redundant ideas that are obsolete, lending credence to the factual rationale, and providing informed perspective to build a society of enlightened minds rather than one built on myth, bias, prejudice, and outdated theories. To change from old approaches may be difficult but the rewards are rooted in perpetual fulfillment (Ezidinma, 2022)

In this book, I intend to divulge knowledge gleaned from various educational resources, share my findings and welcome alternative perspectives, provoke healthy discussions, and exhort a fresh world view. From empirical evidence based on years of association with diverse racial backgrounds, I've concluded that each individual I have met is special in their unique ways when confronted with an open mind and love. In future editions, we shall review ideas in need of modification and expound on current trends necessary to improve our society in terms of living in harmony.

Chapter Four

The role of education in the journey

The saying goes that knowledge is power and that is true. Succinctly stated, education is the gateway to knowledge, which in turn enables individuals to develop skills, and become experts in their chosen field. Education broadens perspectives, world views, analytical ability, reinforces confidence, and enhances the ability to solve both simple and complex problems. In this chapter, I focus on the role of education as the springboard to excel and to pursue the American dream.

Education from a subjective perspective is essential to dismantling illiteracy. Illiteracy, on the other hand, is not only the inability to read and write. but the state of remaining in perpetual isolation from activities and opportunities, like earning a decent income necessary to escape from poverty. Further, education allows for personal development – to adapt and function in a rapidly changing society, as well as to avoid being left behind.

From the inception of my journey, I was expected to possess the minimum level of education to be admitted to the University in the United States. Education provided the foundation which paved the way to attainment of goals designed to achieve success. The role of education in is vital to improve one's socio-economic status. Education also enables us to articulate and understand our duties to ourselves, our family, and society. The journey to achieve the American dream has been driven by the quest for education.

The role of education to function

Education plays a pertinent role in the formation of core values, attitudes, and behavior to grow and pursue bigger dreams. Even with changes in the economic condition, acquiring education has been helpful to adapt, compete, and eventually survive and succeed as well as create employment opportunities for others.

Along the line of the educational continuum, taking classes in various courses contributed to broadening my understanding of different disciplines, enriching essential knowledge and my ability to handle personal, business, and social issues. Continuous education, or what is known as adult education, remains an indispensable approach to keeping abreast with new trends and knowledge.

Lessons gleaned from educational sources emanated from experts who have spent time and effort to put into writing experiences and findings, designed to help us deal with issues of daily living. Interestingly, learning from others with expert opinions – a vital source of education – made it possible for me to develop an awareness of personal capabilities to contribute to the building of a functional U.S. society.

With years of accumulated educational enrichment skills such as networking with people in related professions, I made progress. By taking online course, and networking with knowledgeable individuals, I also made remarkable growth and productive outcomes in building meaningful academic and business relationships. Application of knowledge from academic sources was vital in making informed decisions, as well as engaging in ventures with high potential for financial rewards.

Although acquiring education was quite challenging, it was during those years that I formulated strategies to understand fundamental ideologies and unspoken values necessary to achieve success and embrace the American dream. One of the tenets for personal growth and development stemmed from the popular saying that America is the land of opportunities. The notion of a society where one can pursue their dreams uninterrupted became a stimulus to explore avenues for career opportunities.

Observation

Reflecting on my experiences in pursuing the American dream, I realized that observational learning enhanced the ability to adapt and succeed in the society. Observation has constituted much of my learning experience during the academic years and beyond. Observational learning occurs when an individual learns something from watching another person perform an act. In other words, observation learning suggests that one's environment and others' actions cast much influence on the observer. From the moment a baby opens his or her eyes, the observation process starts. The baby recognizes the primary caregivers, notices the surroundings, and begins to recognize objects around him or her. In the same manner, observation allowed me to learn about behaviors, attitudes, and relationships.

It was easier to learn cultural values – norms, customs and traditions, nonverbal cues, and in particular teamwork – through observation. In the learning process, I decided to practice only those values, attitudes, and behaviors that are positively oriented. As is the case, the United States has cultural values that are uniquely set apart, especially how people interact and treat each other.

For example, during my academic years, and at my workplace, I observed how people greeted each other, the words they used, and their body language. I was moved to learn that people, – even strangers, cared enough to ask me how I was doing. I was influenced positively and recognized that human beings care about each other regardless of the color of their skin or nationality. The lesson here is that in my home country when people meet, they ask similar question – "how are you doing?" – before any conversation takes place. Again, I observed that people used inspiring words to end the interactions such as "have a nice day" or "have a great day." Most of the time it is said with a smile. It was interesting to watch, learn and put into practice such positive observation.

Behavior

To assimilate into the society and accomplish notable goals in terms of achieving the American dream, requires acceptable behaviors in line with the cultural norms. Behavior in the context of learning is to understand what is acceptable and what is not - whether in school, at work, or in society. On that note, people are rewarded and punished based on their behavior. Good behavior attracts accolades, praises, and recognition, while bad behavior is condemned, not tolerated, and discouraged. It is a fact of life that behavior has its consequences. Here is an account of behavior and its consequence.

It didn't take long before I noticed how conscious people are about time. Time defines activities of the day, and wasting time is considered unacceptable behavior. I remember the experience I had with the manager at my first job. I was given the assignment to put an order together for delivery. The list was handed to me, and I went to work on it. It didn't take long before the manager came to check on it. He said, "Is the order ready to go?" I said not yet – a few more minutes. He said look, you need to work on your speed. How we manage time here determines our relationships with our customers. If the delivery is not on time, there will be no repeat business. Some competitors are ready to get the order done on time if we are unable to do so. I picked up on my speed and he was happy about it.

Coming to work late is a serious matter. On several occasions, employees who came to work late were given a warning because it was considered bad behavior. Those who failed to abide by the company's policy to be on time for work were terminated. Before employees are terminated, the company policy is to give them warning to stop coming to work late or else be ready for the consequences.

The manager went further to lecture us why keeping to time is considered a cultural norm. Because of competition in the industry, he said, our competitors would like to capture more market share by serving customers who are not happy with us. It is therefore essential to provide the customer with quality service on time, to make them happy, and by so doing, we have repeat businesses.

In general, the pace at which activities are conducted in society shed light on the importance of time management. It was quite an experience to notice the operations of fast-food restaurants. The essence of it all is about saving time because many people don't have time to cook. Orders are placed and within three to five minutes the order is ready, and the food is consumed as the driver heads to his or her destination. The lessons gleaned from adapting to societal values and norms were helpful to achieving the American dream.

Attitude

Having a positive attitude was helpful in achieving success. Attitude is a mental framework that shapes what we make out of life. Attitude impacts every aspect of our lives. Understanding the pros and cons of attitude helped me to overcome obstacles, barriers, and challenges along the journey. I realized that I have control over my attitude and tried to be on the positive side. For example, when we direct a certain attitude towards someone, instantaneously the same attitude is reflected back to us.

I noticed how people's attitude impacted their mood, behavior, and relationships with others. Our attitude not only affects professional life but also affects our state of well-being. Because attitude matters in the outcome of any endeavor, efforts should be made to ensure that interaction with others is laden with positive attitude. The good news is that we have the choice to make a decision on attitude in any situation. Our attitude is the only barrier standing between us and success (D'Amico, 2016).

To get a better perspective on attitude, it is helpful to examine how it is manifested. Attitude can be exhibited through how we think, walk, talk, uses eye contact, and behave. A positive attitude has many benefits, including:

1. Confidence to try new ways of doing things without fear
2. Increased productivity
3. Happy mood and lots of energy
4. Ability to overcome difficulty with less stress
5. Better relationship with people
6. Optimistic outlook on life
7. Willingness to collaborate and contribute to the common good

On the other hand, negative attitudes manifest in conduct like constant complaining, angry outbursts, constant blaming of others when things go wrong, difficulty working with others, and opinionated attitude. Effects of negative attitude include the following:

1. Hurting innovation, affecting morale, and lowering productivity.
2. Making life difficult for family, coworkers, and customers
3. Health problems
4. When the leader is negative, work becomes boring and unfulfilling
5. Poor performance and failure

From a theoretical perspective, as well as from lessons gleaned from observation, attitude is critical in interpersonal relationships. How individuals act and behave could determine the outcome of any interactions. I observed that greater number of people in the society had attitudes that could be described as upbeat. It was interesting to work in such environment. It was apparent both in the private and business sectors that positive attitude goes a long way to promote positive outcomes.

Likewise, from an observational standpoint, a negative attitude could damage or eliminate any desire for further interaction in private or business matters. Dealing with individuals who are hard to please could be difficult and frustrating. For example, when I worked for one company, a customer walked in to place an order. The cashier said hello, good morning, how are you doing? The customer refused to say a word, then with an angry face said, give me numbers 3 and 6, and how much is it? That type of attitude creates an unfriendly atmosphere. The cashier put a rush on the order and got it ready, handed it to the customer and politely says "have a nice day." You can guess: No response from the customer.

On the other hand, some customers come in with smiling faces. They place their orders and patiently wait to be served. When the order is ready, they are served and with a smile they thank the waiter and express their appreciation for the service. The whole atmosphere is charged with positive energy and people are happy.

The point here is that being exposed to the cultural norms in society could influence our attitude and cause changes to occur, which could also impact who we are. But then, is up to the individual to discern from their observations and incorporate healthy values necessary to succeed and have a positive impact in the society. I have experienced many beneficial outcomes of incorporating positive attitudes along the way to achieving my American dream.

Visual learning

Prior to living in the United States, I watched television in part to enrich my understanding of current events in the country. I watched the news to enrich my understanding of what was going on in the country as well as important events around the world. However, when I came to the United States, I watched television for dual purposes: first to enrich my vocabulary, and second, to learn to improve and communicate more fluently in English. By watching television news, listen to people, watching spots, talk shows, and entertainment programs, I became more acclimated to the culture.

Television became a medium by which the American experience came to life. As a source of learning, it impacted my worldview, triggered my curiosity to explore, and the urge to have big dreams. Research studies have shown that those who watched television as children have the propensity to develop better relations when they became adults (Anderson & Houston, 2001).

In another research study, it was found that individuals who spent time watching educational programs during childhood scored higher in different curricular subjects as well as in specific attitudes (Low & Durkin, 1998). Research data suggest that the television medium promotes a better understanding of virtual images, develops positive attitudes and skills, and increases motivational power, stimulation of imagination, and vocabulary enrichment than verbal communication (Anderson & Houston, 2001).

For most immigrants, television offers an effective source to become acclimated to a new culture and society. Based on research studies, 70% of immigrants improved their understanding of the English language through watching television. In sum, television serves as an educational source to offer a comprehensive understanding of different facets of society. Although social media has been with us for a short while, they are valuable means of communication, exchange of information, and forum for discussions.

Documentaries

I became interested in watching documentaries on television during my leisure time. The documentaries were varied and offered the viewer the opportunity to obtain detailed information on political, business, or social issues. Notable documentaries that gave me "food for thought" were programs addressing the negative impact of segregation, equal rights, the civil rights movement in the United States. The documentaries were captivating, revealing, and informative to say the least.

After watching these documentaries, the questions that came to mind were: What would have been the impact of attending a segregated school? How would I have been impacted by unequal rights? Without the civil rights movement, could I have achieved my educational and professional dreams? I think that it would have been difficult to navigate all the racial barriers to be successful.

I use this medium to express my sincere gratitude to men and women of all racial groups who diligently resisted racism, segregation, and discrimination, through the enactment of laws against such practices. It is much easier to achieve he American dream when there are no barriers and obstacles to navigate.

Chapter Five

Landmark Issues of Concern

Celebrating holidays in the United States reminds me of the historical significance of such events, and the reason to be grateful for all those who have contributed to making life more enjoyable for all of us. One of my favorite holidays is the celebration of United States of America's Independence Day. We were in the backyard celebrating with families. Our neighborhood is racially mixed, so we had some neighbors come over to enjoy the occasion. One of the neighbors said to me "Happy Independence Day." To which I replied, "the same to you." A conversation began. I said to him and his wife that we are blessed to live in the United States with lots of opportunities. Importantly, we talked about the struggle and challenges America has experienced in the past and how things are changing. We talked about the war of independence, the civil war, segregation, civil rights, and how far the cities have developed. Succinctly, we delved into events that shaped this country and expressed our optimistic view for the future of our country.

The conversation was thought-provoking and indelible in my mind. I started to appreciate how the country has always found ways to keep moving forward by dealing with controversial issues through discussions, debates, and the judicial system -- to find common ground. The information from the conversation with my neighbor about the trying times in the country's history, triggered my interest to explore relevant issues that shaped the state of the union, like those that follow.

Housing segregation

By the time I arrived in the United States, housing segregation was almost nonexistent. We lived in a neighborhood with mixed races. I had wondered what it would have been like to experience refusal to live in any neighbor of my choice because of my skin color. I am grateful to those who opposed it and equally grateful that the government intervened to eradicate such divisive practices. Evidence shows that segregation harms people who live in high poverty racially segregated neighborhoods and segregation harms the metropolitan areas at large (Brenner and Pastor, 2015). While whites tend to live in the predominately white area, the trend is changing. According to (Logan and Stulss, 2015), in 1980 the average white person lived in a neighborhood, where 88 percent of the population was white, while in 2010, the average person was living in a neighborhood with 76 percent whites. The high degree of segregation based on race impedes access to education and other public services, the opportunity for social interaction, labor market prospects, and quality of health care.

Segregation limits economic and advancement opportunities. The wealthy living in highly segregated neighborhoods have greater access to resources such as safer neighborhoods, higher home value, quality municipal services, and better schools. Desegregation favors minorities because most can better their economic standards and can afford to improve their standard of living. According to Shaporo & Osoro in a 2013 study, racial segregation and inequity are also negatively associated with African Americans, limiting their capacity to become homeowners and business owners. Again, the point is that segregation has an unhealthy effect on the economic growth in the community. The more I became aware of the negative impact of segregation, the more I realized that it is up to all of us to work with our representatives to take action against it. Being able to buy a house for me and my family in racial mixed neighbor is symbolic of achieving the American dream to which I am grateful to God and our government.

Researchers on segregation (Dreier, 2014) argued that the vicious cycle of sprawl and economic segregation imposes significant costs on all parts of the metro area. Research studies suggest that metro areas with a higher number of residential segregations by race and skill level have shorter economic growth than areas with a low level of segregation. This finding informed us about the adverse impact of segregation on the individual as well as the entire metro area. Although changes are taking place to eradicate housing segregation, it is our civic responsibility to contribute in any way possible to ensure that residential housing is integrated, which is necessary to build a healthy and prosperous society.

School segregation

It was a big step in the right direction to dismantle school segregation because, fundamentally it is a flawed and divisive policy. I have wondered what it would have been like to attend a segregated school or live in a segregated neighborhood. I read about men and women of good conscious who aggressively campaigned against it, took it to the highest court in the land and challenged it, and won. Bravo to all of them. It was a victory for all of us because we are privileged to go to any school of our choice. Segregation meant that schools admit students a long racial line. In other words, the color of one's skin determines the bases for admission to school and buying a house for the family. We need to do better than that.

We are fortunate to attend interracial schools. This is because such schools offer students the opportunity to enrich their academic experience through the exchange of information. In addition, students learn to work together and are better prepared to work as teams, in preparation for actual experience in the society. Desegregation in schools remains a catalyst in terms of promoting equality, teamwork, exchange of information, and enrichment of knowledge from various backgrounds. I learned about desegregation from the civil rights era and wanted to share my perspective to advance justice and fairness. To be able to enroll in any school of one's interest amounts to freedom of choice. On that note, the U.S. Supreme Court patently declared segregation in schools to be unconstitutional in the landmark 1954 ruling Brown Vs Board of Education.

Nonetheless, school segregation continues to exist even after it was declared unconstitutional, and lawsuits against it range on. According to findings, more than half of the nation's students are in a racially concentrated school district school, where 75 percent of the students are either white or nonwhite, even though the abundance of research shows that integration is still one of the available tools to achieve racial equality (Meatto, 2019).

As parents, the issue of segregation is of importance because our children's quality of education is at stake. Although the subject of segregation may be sensitive or uncomfortable to discuss, the negative impact requires that we express our concern and demand equality. The existence of segregation even after it has been declared unconstitutional raises the question of core American values of equality, and fairness.

Evidence indicates that segregation is unfair and marginalizes the quality of education for minorities. Findings indicate that some school districts have more money to spend than others. In one example, a school district that predominately serves students of color received $21 billion less in funding than other, mostly white districts in the United States that serve similar numbers of students (Meatto, 2019).

So, the question becomes, how do we ensure that our children go to better schools that are integrated? In that regard, parents need to take the initiative and chose the schools that are integrated for their children. By attending integrated schools, students are not limited to their community, but rather are exposed to students from other communities which could provide them the opportunity to exchange and gain new knowledge. This is what education is all about – learning from the teacher, from textbooks, and from each other.

The Civil Right Movement

I read with curiosity the activities that shaped the Civil Right movement. The movement was a critical event in the history of the United States. It was a test for democracy, justice, and freedom. The lesson here is that the constitution of the United States if applied correctly is the law of the land that must be venerated. The civil rights movement paved the way for all Americans to understand that the same opportunity exists for everyone to pursue their legitimate dreams in a free society.

What comes to mind when I think about the civil rights movement is the famous speech Martin Luther Jr. in which he said, "I have a dream" and concluded with "we are free at last." Civil rights history is associated with the African American Civil Right movement in the 1950s and 1960s. I was curious to know the details to appreciate the efforts of all Americans who supported the movement.

The primary purpose was to end discrimination and racial segregation which represented American idealism. Great African Americans such as Martin Luther King Jr., Malcolm X, and John Lewis emerged. I became interested in the history of the civil right movement because it offered lessons on the importance of speaking out to demand justice, equality, and fairness. In addition, the nonviolent approach adopted by Dr. King was an ingenious strategy that won him the admiration of the world, and for that reason, he was given the Nobel Peace Prize. The outcomes of the non-violence strategic approach convinced me that it is through peaceful dialogues as exemplified in the civil rights struggle that significant victories can be won. It is a lesson to be engraved in our hearts as a paradigm for future conflict resolutions.

Here we shall focus on the highlight of the civil rights movement to examine the events that led to victory from the Supreme court. These events are significant because they eliminated barriers which would have made it impossible to achieve the American dream.

- On May 17, 1954, the United States supreme court decided on the Brown vs. Board of Education, which ended legal segregation in public schools.
- Rosa Park was arrested for civil disobedience for refusing to give her seat to a white passenger on the city bus. Her arrest led to the desegregation of the Montgomery buses in 1956.
- The Civil Right Act was passed on September 9, 1957, ensuring that African Americans could exercise their constitutional right to vote.
- On February 1, 1960, four black students sat at a white-only lunch counter at Woolworth store in Greensboro North Carolina. Similar sit-ins took place all over the country, eventually causing several store and restaurants to change their practices.
- The march in Washington, DC with thousands in attendance called for the Civil Right Act. On August 27, 1963, Martin Luther King Jr. delivered his famous "I Have a Dream" speech. The nonviolent approach to the march has remained a successful strategy, winning the sympathy of the nation and bringing favorable attention to the civil rights cause.
- President Lydon B. Johnson signed a law making it illegal to discriminate on the bases of color, race, religion, national origin, and gender.

- The 24th amendment of the United States Constitution was ratified on January 23, 1964. The purpose was to allow African Americans to vote.
- The Bloody Sunday was an event organized to protest the murder of Jimmie Lee Jackson, by an Alabama State trooper, also for black voter registration rights. The demonstrators were attacked after they refused to disperse. About 50 people were seriously injured. As a result, many white Americans were angry as they became aware of the injustices that black people suffered.
- On July 2, 1964, United States President Lyndon Johnson signed the Civil Rights Act into law. The purpose was aimed at eliminating legal barriers that prevented African Americans to exercise their right to vote. Several historians regard this law as the most pertinent and effective civil law ever enacted in the United States.
- On the 4th of April 1968, Martin Luther King Jr. was shot and killed at the Lorraine Motel in Memphis Tennessee. King was in Memphis to support a strike of black sanitation workers who were protesting wage discrimination and poor working condition. James Earl Ray was captured and pleaded guilty to the murder.

Retrieved from: African American Civil History Facts. www.black-history-facts-.com/Black-Civil-Right-mo

Chapter Six

Testing the waters – attempts to contribute

For several years, working for different corporations was the norm for me. The decision to go private was made after a friend lost his job because the organization was going through a merger. The organization was bought out and several employees were not needed to continue doing their jobs. For the first time, it occurred to me that I had no control over my job and that I could be laid off at any time. I wanted security for my family and also, and I wanted to be a part of the job-creating sector for economic growth in the United States of America.

The thought of running a private business became more intense the more I learned about people losing their jobs for one reason or the other. At this time there was a recession that lasted for three years, during which job availability was scarce and companies were closing down in record numbers. I had a friend who wanted to move and asked for help. I took it upon myself to arrange for the truck to move the furniture. We went to U-Haul and rented a truck and completed the project within three hours. I realized that it didn't cost much to rent the truck and move the furniture with two men.

Before the move, we had called moving companies to inquire about the cost to move two bedrooms and one sitting room. Comparatively, it was much cheaper to rent the truck and take care of the move. Having analyzed the cost of hiring a moving company and doing it ourselves, it was obvious the amount of money saved. Based on that analysis, we figured out it would be a profitable business to buy a moving truck and hire workers and get into the moving business. The idea was born and implemented, and a moving company was incorporated.

How we got started

The United States of America offers its citizen a fertile environment to participate in business activities with robust potential for success. Reflecting the U.S. constitution, everyone has equal opportunity to engage in a legal business venture, with an unrestricted degree of competitive privilege as well as freedom of speech. The motivation to engage in private business was equally influenced by reading about great American business tycoons such as Henry Ford, Rockefeller, Sam Watson, William Bell, and Thomas Edison, plus other men and women with remarkable business acumen who become successful entrepreneurs.

We operated sales and marketing ventures as well as a moving and storage business before diversifying into the residential and commercial construction industry. No organization, big or small, can succeed without carefully selected employees, who are dedicated to executing the mission, goals, and objectives of the organization. The quality of the employees determines the degree to which productivity and output are generated. A rigorous selection process was utilized to select employees with experience in their respective fields. In addition, these employees could work on their own without constant supervision.

The decision to engage in the private sector was reinforced by stories of those who started with little capital and made it to the top, as long as they were willing to take the risk and bear the consequences. I had a burning desire to achieve the American dream. By observing the business landscape, it was apparent that anyone with the zeal and financial resources could integrate into the business arena.

Although I worked in the corporate world for years my dream was to go private and encounter any challenges and endeavors needed to succeed. Again, I admired the opportunities in the society where jobs can be created by small and big businesses, making it possible for anyone willing to work to find employment. I was also driven by the desire to participate and contribute to the economy as well as provide jobs to individuals to take care of their families.

To go private required time to figure out which industry and the type of business with potential for success and profit. Research studies revealed pertinent information in the market. As a young company, we realized that a niche existed that big companies ignored, and we gladly tapped into it. Again, our passion to serve the market and satisfying our customers energized us to devote more resources to become more competitive. Time and efforts were invested to train our field teams to discharge their duties with an impeachable professional touch.

Our management team deserves the credit for strategizing effective operational guidelines, aligning our goals and objectives with attention to customer service – namely quality service and prompt response to problematic issues. With intense competition in the industry, focusing on customer loyalty and quality services yielded impressive divided in terms of repeat business and referrals. Customer's opinions were solicited which assisted to mitigate errors and enhance efficiency.

Based on research studies generated from customer feedback, we found out that our greater percentage of clients indicated that the rationale for repeat business and referrals stemmed from competitive prices and prompt services. To reward previous customers for their loyalty, birthday cards, holiday cards, and Christmas cards were sent to them annually.

To consolidate our position and generate more income revenues we embarked on expansion initiatives – more branch offices were opened. More resources were needed, and it required more capital investment to ensure a comprehensive business plan. We carried out feasibility studies to select the most profitable cities to open a branch office.

Before offices were opened, we collected relevant data to make informed decisions. Selecting personnel to run various branch offices was given top priority. According to Jack Welch, your organization's performance is only as good as those who run it (2015). During the selection process, several candidates were interviewed for the position and in the end, it was narrowed to three candidates. The final interview was conducted with a focus on the candidate's ability to function without much supervision. We operated a Moving storage business for several years before we discovered a more profitable business in the construction industry and took advantage of it.

Most of my years in the United States have been spent running different businesses. In the course of operating these businesses, valuable knowledge and know-how have been accumulated which could be helpful for anyone interested in becoming an entrepreneur. Presented are pertinent guidelines that if applied effectively could enable anyone to achieve the American dream as an entrepreneur.

Entrepreneurship

The decision to major in business administration and leadership was influenced by the desire to create jobs and contribute to the growth of the economy in the United States. Having acquired education, it became necessary to put it into practice. In that regard, the decision to go into the private sector was made after weighing checks and balances with corporate employment. Both choices have their benefits and downsides, however, it was a matter of selecting the best alternative. Again, having acquired academic and working experience, it was time to become an entrepreneur. This section provides an account of the challenges and triumphs inherent along the way to operating a business organization.

I felt compelled to include decades of business experience to teach and share relevant principles needed to become a successful entrepreneur. Understanding some of the business concepts could be helpful to those who are not sure if they have the skills and capabilities to become self-employed, and to reevaluate their decisions before investing time and financial resources.

An entrepreneur is someone who creates a new business venture and is ready to bear the risk associated with business ownership as well as reap the rewards from the business. We were willing to take the risk and reap the reward when we started the business. The notion is that an entrepreneur is regarded as an innovator, a source of a new idea, goods, services, or a good business leader. The purpose to be an entrepreneur was to play a key role in the nation's economy, by using the skills, and knowledge gleaned from education, and experience, to great jobs. In addition, we wanted to serve the needs of our customers as well as create employment opportunities on all levels of the organization.

It is always pertinent to assess in detail why one wants to become an entrepreneur because such rationale could serve as goals as well as motivating factors. For example, these are possible rationales to go private:

- To be your boss
- To experience creative freedom
- To use acquired skills and knowledge to serve customers
- To become financially independent and reach to those in need
- To play key roles in growing the economy by creating employment opportunities

Risk-taking

Risk-taking meant that the outcome of the business remains unknown. On that note, the entrepreneur is operating under uncertainty, because things could change that may adversely affect the business plan. However, the steps to move the business forward in most cases are based on the notion that the business will be successful.

To get started and avoid failure, an entrepreneur needs to ensure that the following conditions are met –

- **Money.** Without cash, it is impossible to pay for expenses to operate the business. To start a business requires that cash is available, if not funding needs to be initiated. There should be a plan to raise money before the business is established. If seed money is needed, work with venture capital firms. Venture capital firms invest in new companies and make profits if the business becomes successful.
- **Security.** Many people are uncomfortable sacrificing steady income from 9-to-5 jobs to run a new business that may fail or succeed. To avoid the risk, the best approach is to operate the business part-time until it starts making a profit.
- **Competition.** Be ready to compete. Find out what your competitor is doing to attract business. Know their promotional incentives and discount policies. Offering reasonable prices and quality products or service is a great strategy, and it is recommended.
- **Inject ideas.** Try to innovate. Add something new. Create new designs and make some changes if possible.

Before starting the business, I asked myself the following questions. These questions must be answered in honesty to determine the degree of success for the new company. If the answer to most of the questions is no, then you need to address those areas before making the commitment.

- How do I come up with a business idea?
- What steps are involved in developing a business plan?
- Should I build a business from the scratch, buy an existing business, or buy a franchise?

- If I need help, where can I find one?
- How do I compete and succeed?

Becoming a successful entrepreneur requires critical evaluation of personal traits, which come to play when others are involved. Remember you are the leader and manager as well as the role model. Before going into business, ask yourself these questions:

- Are you a self-starter, can you develop, and follow ideas without hesitation?
- Do you get along with different personalities that you encounter and are you willing to make adjustments?
- Are you confident in making difficult decisions in most situations, especially under pressure?
- How would you describe your plan on a scale of 1 to 10?
- Are you prepared to pay the price? This is to say, are you ready to invest time and efforts to conduct the business? Are you ready to work 12 hours or more per day, 6 to 7 days a week, without complaining?
- Have you prepared your family to be aware of your intention to be an entrepreneur, and discuss how it will affect your time, family time, and social activities? Remind them that when the business is established and running smoothly that there will be more family time.

Why small businesses are important to the nation

Small businesses constitute major forces in the United States economy. There are more than 28 million small businesses in the country. Small businesses altogether generate about 54 percent of sales and, 55 percent of jobs in the United States (SBA, U.S. Small Business Administration, 2016). The business world as we know it today is shaped by individuals who started their businesses. According to SBA, a small business is independently owned and operated with fewer than five hundred employees (U.S.B, 2016).

For example, some business founders like Henry Ford, Thermos Edison, and Alexander Graham Bell are immortalized in history as great entrepreneurs. Equally, in modern times, great entrepreneurs include Bill Gates (Microsoft), Warren Buffet (Investor), Steve Jobs (Apple), Jeff Boozes (Amazon), Sam Walton (Wal-Mart), and Larry Page and Sergey Brin (Google). These entrepreneurs have remarkably impacted the world of business as they continue to grow and innovate. I cited these successful entrepreneurs to exhort anyone eager to start a business that the dream could be achieved successfully.

Besides contributing to the economy, small business founders contribute to the growth and vitality in specific areas, in terms of socioeconomic development such as job creation, and the opportunity for individuals to achieve financial success and independence. That the United States is a wealthy country - admired all over the world, stems from the fact that entrepreneurship is encouraged by the government, allowing individuals to become innovative – to develop products and services, which in turn create job opportunities. As individuals earn income, they can afford necessities and enjoy a better standard of living.

Job Creation

What excites me as an entrepreneur is the opportunity to create jobs – hiring enthusiastic people, working together to satisfy the customer, and seeing the business succeed. The majority of U.S. workers are employed in small businesses. Small businesses often hire more frequently and fire frequently than do big businesses (Headd, 2019). Because small businesses need workers, hiring takes place frequently. However, survival is uncertain, as many small businesses close and workers lose their jobs. But over time, more jobs are created by small businesses which results in a net increase in employment. A strong economy encourages individuals to start entrepreneurship, which was the case when we started. The economy was booming, people were working and, demand for products and services was on the high end. In a weak economy, the opposite is the case. In weak economy, demand for products and services are down, sales are down, and consequently, employees lose their jobs when the organization is not generating profit from production.

Innovation

Part of our competitive strategy was through an innovative approach. We were able to introduce new designs, utilized organic materials to appeal to environmentally friendly customers, and install water-saving devices. Although big businesses have large financial resources to introduce new products, according to the SBA, small businesses develop more patents per employee than do big businesses. In the recent four years, large companies generated 1.7 patients per hundred employees, while small companies generated an impressive increase of 28.5 patients per 100 employees (Breitzman & Hicks, 2008). Over the years, the list of important innovations by small firms includes airplanes, electricity, air conditioning, and DNA fingerprinting. In terms of innovation, small business owners are likely to find new ways of doing things. For example, in 1994, a young science computer graduate working on Wall Street came up with the idea of selling books on the internet. During his first year of selling books on the internet, Jeff Booze's sales from the new company reached half a million dollars. In less than twenty years, annual sales had topped $107 billion (Yahoo.com).

In addition, not only did Boozes innovation in online retailing made him exceedingly rich the effort established a viable model for the eCommerce industry. Small companies are innovative because they intend to always improve the way things are done. In that regard, big organizations are now learning from small businesses. Several big organizations have downsized, to act more like small companies. Several large organizations have now many work units with the intent to spark innovation (Skripak, 2016). People working in these units focus their attention to develop new products and the parent company does the promotion and marketing.

Opportunities for women and minorizes

To fully live the American dream entails becoming responsible citizens. For example, we need to give back to the community, the United States, and our country of origin. More women and minorizes are becoming entrepreneurs, and that is encouraging because it has a positive impact on the economy.

According to Skripak (2016), operating small businesses is the channel through which women and minorities can enter the economic mainstream, achieve financial success as well as feel a sense of accomplishment. This type of mindset motivated me to become an entrepreneur.

Interestingly, while many businesses are owned by white males, during the past two decades there has been a substantial increase in the number of women and minority businesses. Fortunately, opportunities are still available for those who are willing to take the risk and establish their businesses. Anyone can do it. We live in a free society and the constitution guarantees us equal right to pursue our dreams to succeed and be happy. The caveat here is: Be prepared to do what it takes.

Why small businesses fail

It is important to present a balanced perspective on becoming an entrepreneur. From my experience and knowledge gleaned over the years, not everyone that goes into business is successful. In this section, there are pitfalls that entrepreneurs ought to watch out for to increase their chances of success. To be successful requires careful planning. I like to share my experience in this regard with the following statements. Failure can be avoided when pitfalls are eliminated by paying attention to diligence. It is a rewarding practice to listen to experts in the type of business you are interested to run. Asking questions could assist to avoid costly mistakes and enhance successful outcomes.

Our mantra to avoid failure was simply this: Take care of the customer, provide quality products or services at a reasonable price. Take a look at the malls or shopping centers and you will notice vacant shops that are closed because they are not generating enough profit. This happens to all types of businesses if business principles are not implemented correctly. Going into business could be risky, but failure could be avoided with sound planning. By investing time to structure the business properly an entrepreneur could be spared from stress, depression, and loss of capital.

Before going into business, I conducted research studies to increase the degree of success because I heard much about business failures. Here are the statistics to expatiate the failure rate of small businesses. According to Stirpak (2016), one out of three businesses goes out of business within the first two years. Half of the small businesses go out of business within two to three years, and about 60 percent and 70 percent don't make it past the seventh year. That said, some industries are worse than others. On that note, our recommendation to anyone interested in going into business is to avoid risky industries. Here are some rationales some experts suggest for small businesses failure.

- **Bad business ideas.** When the idea is flawed or unrealistic it becomes difficult to implement the business plan. For example, operating a business in a location with little demand for the product or service is a recipe for failure.
- **Cash problem.** Lack of cash available to handle bills and contingencies could be dexterous and lead to business failure. When little money is coming in and lots of it is going out, it becomes difficult to make a profit, and without profit, the result is failure. I have seen this happens in so many businesses.

74

- **Lack of managerial skill.** When the owner lacks managerial experience and skills, it could lead to poor decision making — a lack of planning, low accountability, and little attention to employees' needs.
- **Bad customer relations.** As I stated previously, the customer is the king and needs to be served with respect, or else they are gone and will never come back. That results in loss of business and revenue which could lead to business failure. One customer that is unfairly treated could talk to about 50 people about the mistreatment, which could hurt the image of the business negatively, and result in business failure.
- **Slow to make changes.** When the business is experiencing an increase in sales and the owner doesn't plan for expansion and hires more workers to meet demand, customers may feel ignored and unhappy. When such is the case customers will switch to other businesses to meet their needs. This could cause the business to fail.

How to get help

Several individuals want to start but the fund to get started becomes the obstacle. Help is available for prospective and existing small business owners. In our case, the business was funded through owner's equity. In this section, we shall share with you how you can obtain funding if you qualify. The possibility to achieve the American dream became a reality with the knowledge of funding opportunities, as well as through owner's equity. We live in a country where the government takes into consideration the welfare of small businesses and makes available funding opportunities for those willing to work hard and achieve their dreams. The government understands that small businesses contribute to growing the economy. When businesses are opened, owners create employment opportunities, hire workers who earn income to take care of their families, as well as pay their taxes to the government.

The Small Business Administration (SBA) has been instituted to assist individuals who want to operate businesses. Although SBA wouldn't loan you the money, it will assist you in getting the loan from a local bank with a guaranteed loan option. So, the first step is to apply for a loan preferably from your bank. A bank officer will decide if the bank will loan you the money. If the loan is not possible, SBA will step in to assist through a loan guarantee. The government reimburses the bank for its losses for up to the amount of the loan guarantee if the loan defaults.

Other programs exist which are available for individuals to start a business. However, before you apply for funding you will have a business plan. Equally, someone at SBA will address your questions on management and technical issues and guide you in the process. The Small Business Development Center (SBDC) also assists current and prospective business owners with business problems and provides free training on management skills (U.S. Small Business Administration, 2016). Achieving the American dream is possible for anyone who pursues it with determination and resolve.

Chapter Seven

Raising the family

The role of the family is central in the pursuit of the American dream. As in every culture, the family is the foundation of the country. Having a family is encouraged to prepare future generations to take over from their parents and to keep the nation from extinction. The family structure is indispensable to train and nurture children for their future role. Such roles include keeping the country moving forward, preparing to achieve the American dream, and maintaining their cultural identity. In this chapter, I provide guidelines for how parents need to work together with their children to remain culturally aware of their heritage (customs and traditional) as well as integrate in the American culture.

Our family worked together to ensure that the children were taken care of and provided with adequate support to focus on their education. As in any relationship, there were healthy discussions about world affairs and how technology has narrowed the world into a global village. With modernization of the telephone system, our children are able to talk to relatives in Nigeria, as well as participate in zoom video calls.

We lived in a neighborhood that is racially mixed – Caucasians, African Americans, Latinos, Asians, and some from the Islands. It was an integrated and friendly neighborhood. During the summer, children played in the park while parent engaged in conversation with their neighbors. Young men and some elder men organized soccer matches to entertain their families.

We were blessed with neighbors who cared for each other. During holiday seasons such as Christmas and Thanksgiving, we exchanged gifts and greeting cards. It was not uncommon to observe a neighbor helping another neighbor to unload furniture or trim tree branches or cut down a tree. Everyone tried their best to show respect towards each other. Why not? Such gestures are needed to create a loving environment and racial harmony.

Having children exacerbated family responsibilities. The children attended public schools. We were invited to PTA meetings. On weekends during the summer, we accompanied the children to the school premises to practice. Watching the children play elicits the childhood in the parents. During game days we rooted for our children's teams, and we had lots of fun participating in cheering season.

Being a parent to children born in the United States by African parents could be challenging. As the children grew up in age, they asked more questions about their heritage, wanting to know more about their ancestry. After homework and assignments were completed, we talked about issues that mattered to them -- conversations with classmates, friends, and highlights of what the teacher said about major topics of the day.

Children In Immigrants Families

As immigrant parents, our core desire for our children is to acquire quality education from early age until they graduate from higher institutions. To provide them with the opportunity to excel, there are challenges and obstacle that need to be removed to create a smoother pathway to actualize successful outcomes.

It was reported that children in immigrant families account for nearly 24 percent of all the country's children in 2010, and a majority of 88 percent are U.S. citizens (Hernandez, & Cervantes, 2021). It was also found that children of immigrants account for the entire growth in the U.S. child population between 1990 and 2008. The well-being of children is especially important to the country because they are the fastest growing segment of U.S. population. Whether they achieve social integration and economic mobility depends on the degree to quality education from preschool to college (Tienola and Haskins 2011).

Citizenship

The vast majority of children in immigrant families about 88 percentage are U.S. citizens, by virtue of being born in this country. It is not surprising because many immigrants arrive during their early adult years, to work, live and raise their families, although they may or may not bring their children with them, most of their child bearing years occurs after they have immigrated and settled in the adopted home land (Tienola and Haskins, 2011). Several immigrant youths as U.S. citizens share precisely the same privileges as children born in in this country.

Recent research indicates that naturalization is increasing exponentially. Between 1990 and 2005, among legal foreign residents, those who became naturalized climbed from 38 percent to 52 percent (Passel, 2017). In consideration of the statistics as a whole, citizenship for the children can be complicated in immigrant families. Thirty percent of children in immigrant families, 6.8 percent of all children, have an undocumented parent of which 1.5 percent of these children themselves are unauthorized to work.

Language challenge

Being fluent in English is critically important in order to participate fully in the society. For those who are challenged with English language, both parents and children are encouraged to learn English language to be able to succeed in school, workplace, and other settings. Although all children in immigrant families have one foreign born parent, about 82 percent of those children speak English fluently. Most children who speak English very well are likely to become bilingual and such children can easily integrate easily in the society and become successful (Passel, 2017). I came from a country where English is the official language, and it was instrumental to facilitate the ability to integrate and assimilate in the society.

Making Polices to Assist Every Child in America

Polices that support working families and invest in the health, economic security and education of all children are important component of national agenda necessary to improve our children's well-being in America. As indicated by research study, both children of immigrants and native-born children with low-income face similar challenges. However, it must be noted that the same policies and programs aimed at helping children in low-income families can present significant barriers to children in immigrant families, when issues such as language and immigration status are not specifically well defined (Cervantes, & Lincroft, 2010).

Children of Immigrants and Healthcare

Taking care of the health of our children is important to ensure they are healthy enough to develop into productive members of the society, and ready to serve our country when needed. To work towards the health care of immigrant children, Congress has to focus on pertinent legislation to improve access and coverage for the children. Despite these initiatives, the needs of immigrant families especially those in low income have been ignored (Tienola & Huskins, 2011).

While the Children's Health Insurance Program Reauthorization Act passed in 2009, and the Affordable Care Act passed in 2010, it included key provisions to improve the health and well-being of millions of children in low families, yet it will be limited for children in immigrant families because they have significant barriers in having health care coverage. In addition, unauthorized immigrant children are four times likely to lack insurance and more likely to lack source of care except going to the emergency room (Tienola & Huskins, 2011)

The passage of the Act was a great victory in making health care more affordable to low-income families as well as including important provisions to streamline enrollment processes accessible to vulnerable population including immigrants. Again, despite important gains, the ACA falls short of closing the health disparity gap for many immigrant children and families. Given this existing gap, it is expected that many immigrant children and families will have to rely on emergency care as well as public hospitals, health centers and clinics to provide affordable health care regardless of the ability of immigrant families to pay.

According to Tienola and Huskins, to truly provide insurance coverage for all children, health insurance coverage must be provided to all children regardless of their immigration status without exception, including unauthorized children because they are at risk of getting worse when they are sick and have no control over where they are born.

Children of immigrants and nutrition support

Food safety programs play important role in meeting the healthy development of children in low-income families. Children of immigrants can be at risk of living in food insecure household than those living in native born households. Research showed that immigrants who are in the country less than five years are 145 percent more likely to become food insecure than U.S.-born families. The high rate of poverty and food insecurity among immigrant families are possible reasons why there is decline in the health outcome among children of immigrants over time.

Although many working low-income families can utilize income-based food safety net programs such as the Supplemental Nutrition Assistance Program (SNAP), immigrant families including those with U.S. citizen have lower rate of enrollment in SNAP. The reason being that immigrants' families don't access such programs due to language and cultural barriers; many distrust government agencies and some encounter challenges in submitting required paperwork. In addition, some immigrants are confused about eligibility rules for the assistance programs.

How racism hurts immigrant children

Immigrant children have their own share of problem dealing with racism. To be able to achieve the American dream it is important to eliminate behaviors that impede advancement opportunities to any child in the country. Children are quick to talk about how their friends and teachers treat them at school. It was a privilege to listen to the children, to understand what bothered them in dealing with classmates regarding racial issues. Immigrant children with heavy accent are likely to be ridiculed or disrespected. Although some immigrant children may speak without accent, on the other hand, children from parents who are not fluent in English may have problem speaking fluent English, which could limit their participation in conversation with their classmates and in the class.

Nurturing immigrant children to grow up and integrate in the society constitutes a milestone worthy of achievement for parents. For this reason, I encourage parents to dedicate sufficient quality time, to find out if any racial behavior is dictated from the teacher or fellow classmates.

For children to become aware of their heritage, parents need to teach them cultural values, norms and why they should be proud of their traditions and customs. This includes knowing their family trees to build up self-confidence. Children who are conversant with their heritage are likely to develop stronger self-identity which is necessary to rebuff racism. Knowledge of the family tree exposes children to understand who their relatives are, the birthplace of their parent's family linage and pertinent cultural values.

Research studies indicate that racism hurts children in a lot of ways. both in their health during adult life and by lessening their chances of being successful in their carrier (McCarthy, 2020). Due to the negative effect of racism on children, there is a call for action to create brighter future for our children. The fact is that biologically all humans are one race, 99 percent of our genes are alike, no matter what color of our skin or what part of the world we come from. Out of greed, power and control, some people have historically found ways to oppress people because of their race (McCarthy, 2020).

Despite our sameness, racism still flourishes because people continue to look for difference to claim superiority and take advantage of others. Racism and its effect can lead to chronic stress for children and chronic stress can lead to actual changes in the hormone that causes inflammation in the body (McCarthy, 2020). Because many immigrants live in fear of financial needs, unemployment and undocumented issues, there is stress in the family which could affect the children. Children raised in African American homes, Hispanics, and American Indian homes are more likely to live in homes with high unemployment, lower income than white children. In that regard they are less likely to have good education, nutrition and living condition. This type of environment could cause some health problem.

National Center for Education noted that in the 2015-2016 school year, 88 percent of white seniors graduated from high school, in comparison only 76 percent of Asian Americans and 79 percent of Hispanics. This statistic is important in terms of economic opportunities and health. It is known that adults with college degree live longer and have lower rates of chronic disease than those who didn't graduate from college (McCarthy, 2020).

To eradicate discrimination and racism for immigrant children and for others. here are suggested steps (McCarthy, 2020).

1. We need to change the way we talk to each other as individuals and as a group.
2. It is important we take a look at ourselves, take a stock of our believe and biases and work to change them.
3. Speak up when we see or hear racist remarks.
4. We need to talk to our children about racism and teach them healthier way of thinking about others and work on our issues with racism.
5. We need to work to stop institutional racism, enforce laws to guide against them.
6. We need to work with our schools to ensure that all children no matter their backgrounds have access to quality education.
7. There should be program in place to help people who are struggling with poverty to participate in becoming productive.
8. Our laws must protect all people not just one group.

This is about the future of our children and our children are our future.

Why cultural education is imperative

My cultural background was helpful in building self-confidence and positive self-identity. United States is described as a melting pot country because people from all over the globe came to this land to participate and make it their home. In so doing, they bring along their customs, traditions, and ways of life. Culture is alive and well and is celebrated all over the country through dance, food, clothing, crafts, and arts.

The first time I felt at home and appreciated living in the United States was when I watched African dance during the summer at a festival organized in Denver. The experience brought back memories of events organized in my village to celebrate various specials occasions. I reflected on amazing drummers, kalimba and shakere players, who displayed unbelievable dancing moves.

I was part of the movement to keep African culture alive in the United States because it is pertinent for every race to preserve their cultural heritage as a reminder of their roots. Our company, Emis African products Unlimited, imported African products such as musical equipment, arts and crafts plus clothing designed with both modern and handmade fabrics from regional African countries.

Over the years, African culture increasingly gained grounds and became popular because it is inclusive-oriented and appeals to people of all ages. The COVID-19 pandemic slowed the pace of growth as it became impossible to gather and celebrate. It is encouraging that educational institutions have departments that provide studies on African culture.

The role of parents to preserve the culture

The lives of most immigrants are influenced by the memories of the world they left behind, as well as the day-to-day struggles of learning to cope with the new society. For example, learning to speak a new language and working with strangers with unfamiliar culture are some of the challenges immigrants have to face. Holding tight to my culture played pivotal role to build my self-confidence and to know that every culture is unique and should be respected.

Attention to cultural awareness is critical as it relates to individual identity and should be treated as a priority to exhort cultural pride to both children and adults. In the early 2000s, we were involved in teaching African cultural programs. Our cultural group went to schools and Universities and participated in cultural events, celebrated with lectures on African cultural history, music, food, and fashions. Teachers and students were encouraged to get involved in African fashion shows and it was a lot of fun for everyone, especially for those who have not participated in African cultural programs.

Cultural awareness and tradition play pertinent roles in helping children develop sense of belonging, solidifying their identity of whom they are and improving their self-esteem. Cultural awareness contributes to build positive self-image. In addition, individuals who are exposed to diverse cultural experiences as children have better social network.

There are several ways parents can teach their children to learn about their culture and explore other cultures:

Learn other languages: Children who are bilingual have advantages because language is a powerful tool to communicate and learn new skills, build productive relationships, and become successful. Being bilingual allows children to bound with relatives and relate better with their cultural background. Learning multiple languages promotes an over-all sense of cultural appreciation and imbues exploration of other cultures.

Celebrate holidays and traditions: Most cultures all over the world celebrate holidays and special occasions. By engaging children to celebrate traditional holidays they are likely to learn about the culture, understand the history behind the celebration, get to know that other cultures exist.

Share stories of family history: Parents could talk about the family linage through generations, highlighting major accomplishments by family members, overcoming challenges, and citing names of popular artists which could stimulate cultural interest in children. By helping children to explore their family tree, it allows them to discover their linkage and connection to the past. When children learn about their family history, they learn about the diversity of talents in their family which helps them to develop an understanding of individual identity.

Using photographs is a great tool to teach children about family trees because they can see and understand the identity of their relatives. With photographs children develop more interest in their family history which could boost their self-image.

Explore new cultures: Getting to learn new cultures provide children the opportunity to explore other cultures, discover diverse lifestyles customs and traditions and to gain new perspective about the world. Various approaches exist to encourage children to explore new cultures. For example, children can learn about other cultures by watching foreign moves, listening to cultural music, and participating in cooking ethnic meals from other cultures. There are several approaches parents could adopt to imbue knowledge of cultural values for their children. Any parent could get started with these suggestions and perhaps try other alternatives. It is important to seek input from children to get involved in the discussion.

Travel to the country of origin: Taking children to visit their parental homeland affords them the opportunity to meet their relatives and distant relatives. It is a powerful approach to instill family and traditional values to their heritage. Such an approach could influence life-long memory of ancestry homeland and exhorts them for more visits. Equally such visits may get them to know the family tree, learn stories about their ancestors, powerful leaders, men and women who have made remarkable contributions in the land. Memories of such trips are indelible. They may want to take their children back home when they become parents.

Storytelling: With modern technology, it becomes much easier to reinforce stories with pictures, videos, and books. Children like to listen to stories about important historic events in the country. It could be stories about independence, festivals celebrating new season, or remembering great warriors and wrestlers. You could talk about the development in the villages, how the landscape has changed from one style to the current style. How people lived in the past compared with the modern closed communities.

Cultural events: It is easier to find cultural events within cities during the summer months. Before the recent pandemic, cultural festival events were published by organizations dedicated to promoting cultural awareness and charitable outreach. The internet is a good source for such contacts. Children can learn a lot by attending cultural festivals where they are exposed to cultural dances, arts, and crafts, traditional food, and ethnic clothes. Such activities are sources of cultural awareness, which could influence positive ethnic pride.

Some festivals have areas where children could enroll to learn about the customs and traditions of the home country and understand how they can go on tours to the home country. Besides, flyers and pamphlets are available, from different organization who are engaged in various cultural activities for promotional purposes.

Learning the language: To speak the native language is a powerful approach in trying to learn the culture. It demonstrates acute interest to understand the customs, and traditions. Embracing the culture triggers heritage pride and enhances bounding with others from the same culture. To speak and understand a native language with fellow tribal members creates an atmosphere of oneness and a sense of family ties.

Watch ethnic movies: Most African countries have film makers who focus on cultural stories and traditions. For example, in Nigeria films are made which depict traditional heritage with historic contents. They feature scenes with actors and actresses engaged in family issues – conflict resolution, marriage ceremonies, coronation events, talk shows, and cooking lessons with ethnic herbs.

Read cultural books and magazines: Magazines and books are great sources to obtain cultural information. With advance technology, databases can be accessed. With a thorough search on Google, books and magazines with focus on culture are available. Children should be encouraged to spend time to glean cultural information about their homeland. Internet searches for cultural information is a formidable alternative to enrich cultural heritage. Another approach in terms of generating children's interest in culture is to encourage them to write class papers and assignments based on their culture. Not only that they will complete the assignment it gives them the opportunity to expand their interest on cultural issues.

Cooking: Inviting children in the kitchen when cooking traditional meals, creates an opportunity for bonding, and for cultural conversation. It is also a time to talk about special recipes--where they are imported from, part of the native country they are grown, and why they are used during special cultural occasions. Cooking traditional food together as a family could be a lot of fun as well as an opportunity to share information on culture. During such session's parents could talk when such meals are prepared -- meals for holidays, birthdays and to celebrate traditional events. Children could be assigned to do the pre work, ask questions about where the food stuffs were imported from. It is also recommended to allow the children to fix some dishes and learn from experience. Ethic foods are growing in popularity because they serve as a vital link to cultural heritage for both parents and children. Ethnic food stores and restaurants are ubiquitous in several cities in the United Sates, and most are on the internet listings.

African Clothes: Listed below are popular African fabrics. African fabrics especially traditional fabrics are available online and some could be imported from regional African countries.

Table 1: African Fabrics

Fabric Name	Country of Origin	Remark

Kente	Ghana	Design and produced by the Osajefo tribe
Asoke Akwaete	Nigeria Nigeria	Designed and produced by the Yoruba tribe Design by Obobo tribe
Mud cloth	Gambia	Design by Dimka tribe
Shamma	Ethiopia	White cotton fabric used to make men and women clothing
Shweshwe	South Africa	Traditional cotton fabric dyed with geometric pattern

Kente: One of the most popular fabrics from Africa comes in four distinct colors. It is a traditional fabric worn by men and women during ceremonial occasions. Men wrap it around their bodies. Women use it as a wraparound shirt. African Fashion designers utilize Kente fabric for various western style clothes.

Asoke: Asoke is made with intricate woven fabric. It is produced by the Ijabu tribe, in Abeokuta area. It is flashy. Asoke is worn for ceremonial occasions such as coronation and royal weddings. The picture below shows men and women in Asoke attire worn during wedding party. It is an ideal fabric for western style outfits.

Mud cloth: Taking its name from the materials used to make it, the fabric is made with white cotton treads dipped in dye made from brown sand. After the fabric is dried, African motifs are drawn on it with indigo ink. Indigo liquid is extracted from crushed indigo seed. Mud cloth fabrics are ideal for making jackets, winter coats, and for table coverings.

Shweshwe: This one is made with white fabric dyed with indigo and has geometric patterns. The fabric is part of South African culture. It is used to design women clothing, especially for women from the Xhosa tribe. It is also used to design men's long sleeve and short sleeve shirts. Most prominent color are indigo, red and brown.

Arts and crafts: African arts and crafts are rooted in explanatory representation of meaningful ideas, stories, relationships, beauty, life, and death. African arts and crafts are utilized by African artists to immortalize important leaders, landmarks, victorious and celebratory occasions. Arts and crafts are equally utilized for decorative purposes as well as symbolic expression of cultural heritage.

Arts and crafts provide us with rich information on our customs and traditions. Interestingly the United States of America is replete with immigrants from all over the world, each with its unique cultural heritage. This is the reason U.S., is admired as the most diversified country in the world.

Chapter Eight

The Impact of Education on Immigrant Families

The degree to which immigrant children are prepared to assimilate into society and participate in the workforce is dependent on a sound background in education. In this regard, parents and the educational system have responsibilities for the education and development of immigrant children. Children from immigrant parents are increasingly part of the U.S. child population, and they will make America their homeland. Their health and educational development as well as future social and economic integration will play significant role in the nation's future. To ensure bright future for immigrant children, it is important to create a conducive environment both at home and in school. The goal in this regard is to provide them access to social programs and educational resources needed for them to develop into mature adults, ready to support themselves, their families and to become productive citizens. equipped to serve their country when needed.

Immigrants and their children who enter postsecondary colleges are likely to become more successful than those who drop out or stop at the high school level (Teramishi, Suarez-Orozco, and Suarez-Orozco, 2011). Most immigrants' parents are known to emphasize the importance of attending college after graduating from high school. Immigrant parents, just like other parents encourages their children to attend higher institutions to increase their chances of getting better jobs and earn attractive salaries.

Post-Secondary Education

Education paves the way to achieve the American dream. I benefited by going to community college as an immigrant. Community colleges offer accessible and affordable post-secondary education that accommodates many needs of immigrant students. To obtain a certificate or associate degree from a community college is necessary to achieve economic mobility. In 2008, for example, adults with some college or associate degree experienced unemployment rates that were about half of those who didn't complete high school. Those who attended college made more money than those with only a high school diploma. Such data underscore the importance of community colleges for access to good jobs, in an economy that is always creating more jobs that require post-secondary education or training.

Most immigrants who came into the country are proficient in the English language. Those who entered the U.S. education system at an early age are well-acclimated to the culture and speak English fluently. It was found that immigrants with high school diploma are more likely than native-born students of the same racial or ethnic group to enroll in any form of post-secondary education (Teramishi, Suarez-Orozco, and Suarez-Orozco, 2011).

Many immigrant students have great financial needs but often lack information on how to finance college costs. They are less likely than native-born to apply for student loans – they borrow less and cover more of their cost by themselves (National

Center for Education Statistics). While naturalized citizens and legal permanent residents are eligible for in-state - tuition, non-permanent immigrant students are treated differently, and they are required to pay high tuition for their education. It is important to increase awareness of financial aid information for immigrant students, to help them access available funds. Even though immigrant students have greater financial needs than native-born students, many of them ignore to seize the opportunity to apply for financial aid. Given the lack of relevant information on the availability of financial aid, there is a need to create more awareness of eligibility to obtain financial aid for the immigrant student. Such awareness initiative should aim to assist immigrant students to navigate and complete the application form correctly before submission (Connell, 2008).

Financial aid poses a particular challenge for undocumented immigrants and their children. In 1990, states began to impose residency that disqualified undocumented immigrants from in-state tuition rates and financial aid. Section 505 of the Federal Illegal Immigration Responsibility Act of 1996 specified that unauthorized aliens "shall not be eligible based on residence (or political subdivision) for any post-secondary education benefits unless a citizen or national of the United States is eligible for such a benefit."

Dealing with Language Barrier

The ability to understand and speak fluently in English is critical for any student to derive maximum knowledge from a college education. To participate in the classroom, in the workplace, or in society requires English proficiency, and some immigrants who are not able to understand or communicate in English are at disadvantage, and often denied the opportunity to secure well-paying jobs. Many immigrants who lack English proficiency in community colleges are encouraged to enroll in English as a Second Language (EASL).

English as a second language course provides immigrants with a range of benefits in addition to the development of skills, confidence in communication, and the ability to secure better-paying jobs. Providing immigrants access to high-quality English language programs would require community leaders and government policymakers to fund high-quality English instructors to manage the program.

High-intensity language programs could allow student to learn outside the classroom by using different curricula to meet the need of various types of immigrant students. To facilitate learning the English language, two options are available. First, community colleges should embark on hiring an ESL facility that is certified to effectively teach the class. Second, community colleges should provide counseling orientation to determine the level of English proficiency and how much time immigrant students need to complete the course.

Challenges to Acquire Education

In sum, immigrant' students face challenges and barriers which hinder their academic and mental development and could affect their progress. Several immigrants juggle academic responsibilities with financial and family responsibilities which could be burdensome. In addition, some immigrants undergo long periods of separation from their parents, which results in stress, anxiety and depression, and withdrawal. To remedy the situation, immigrant students and their families would be better served by counselors who are trained to address the specific needs associated with immigration.

Paying attention to challenges encountered by immigrants and their families in pursuit of educational achievement is an investment laden with huge potential. With greater attention and responsiveness to immigrants in post-secondary and higher institutions, immigrants would be more productive and contribute to the society. Providing financial support to immigrants to complete their education will not only result in personal gain for immigrants and their families but equally benefits our nation in terms of greater productivity and economic growth.

The Role of Higher Education for Immigrants and their Families

Success in higher education translates into bright future for immigrants, which in turn confers benefits to society as a whole (Baum & Flores, 2011). With the increasing demand for skilled labor and educated professional in the U.S., the country will benefit by allowing immigrants access to higher education. In consideration of the increase in the immigration population, policymakers and educators need to focus on increasing immigrants' participation in higher education to ensure greater participation for in the economy.

Lack of familiarity with the U.S. higher education system is a challenge for immigrants, especially for those whose parents are not proficient in English. Applying for college and financial aid could be a complex task even for those whose parents are college graduates.

Research studies indicate that immigrants as well as their children have higher rate of post-secondary educational attainment than native-born Americans (Baum & Flores, 2011). Some researchers argue that the immigrant advantage is a result of "positive selection" – that immigrants from all countries tend to have a higher level of human capital and motivation, which is typical in their country of origin. Immigrants tend to encourage and support each other to pursue higher education.

It is noted that considerable evidence indicates that immigrants from all countries are positively selected from their national population and those who enter the country are among the best educated in their country and are highly skilled. Even when they enter the U.S., they have a high rate of graduation from higher institutions. Researchers noted that significant differences in educational outcomes of immigrant groups could be attributed to pre-immigration characteristics and experiences. In order words, how they progress in education is influenced by their attitude toward positive selection.

It is important to mention that efforts have been made to increase the number of undocumented immigrants in post-secondary education.

Having a good education is critical for social mobility. Enrollment in higher education is increasingly tied to the labor market in the United States. Having a degree from a four-year college offers many advantages and brings significant rewards. Adults with bachelor's degrees earn 50 percent more a year than their counterparts with only a high school education. For those with an associate degree, the difference is about 30 percent. The benefits of higher education are not all monetary; college graduates have broader carrier choices. They prepare their children better for educational opportunities and tend to have a lifestyle with greater health and longevity (Baum & Payea, 2010).

Immigrants face the same similarities of barriers to enrolling in higher education, and such barriers should not be ignored. Even though immigration has become such a divisive issue in the United States, it is more pertinent to focus on the benefits to the society of an open-door policy for immigrants to higher education. This approach is a better strategy than adopting a lock-door strategy. Given the increasing roles, immigrants will play in the American economic future, it is prudent to encourage young people to have access to higher education through financial aid, grants, and scholarships.

Policies aimed to place barriers to improving post-secondary and high education attainment should be eradicated to increase the number of immigrant graduates in society. Given that the young immigrants are the fastest growing groups in the population, the urgency to find favorable policies to facilitate their enrollment into higher institutions is of much importance.

Making Progress through Education

The journey to live the American dream is evident. Immigrants from sub-Saharan countries make up the majority of

African immigrants, and most have been able to achieve the American dream all over the country. Here we present relevant information on their progress – demographics, educational attainment, participation in society, transnational activities as well as challenges encountered to assimilate into the new homeland.

Approximately 2 million Sub-Saharan African immigrants (SSAI) live in the United States of America as of 2018. This population is relatively small, representing just 4.5 percent of the country's 44.7 million immigrant population. Between 2010 and 2018, The Sub-Saharan African immigrant population increased by 52 percent, much higher than the 12 percent increase for the overall foreign-born population. By the year 1980, there were 150,000 residents from sub–Saharan African countries in the United States. Since the '80s, there have been huge immigrants from sub-Saharan countries such as Nigeria, Ethiopia, Ghana, Somalia, and South Africa.

Overall, there are more than 2 million immigrants from 51 countries that make up sub-Saharan Africa, representing 84 percent of the 2.4 million African immigrants. The rest are from the six countries of North Africa – Algeria, Egypt, Morocco, Sudan, and Tunisia (United Nations Population Division, 2017). As of 2018, 81 percent of sub-Saharan African immigrants living in the United States are from East and West Africa. More than half of sub–Saharan African immigrants are naturalized U.S. citizens, and most of the 97,800 who obtained legal permanent residence (green card) in 2017 arrived as immigrant relatives of U.S. citizens, refugees, or through the Diversity Lottery program. In comparison to the total foreign population in the United States, sub-Saharan Africans are better educated, participate in the labor force at a high rate, and are more likely to speak English. (International Immigration Stock, 2017).

Sub-Saharan African Immigrants' locations

Sub-Saharan African immigrants tend to spread throughout the United States. As of 2013 -2017, the states with the largest shares of sub-Saharan African immigrants were Texas (11 percent), New York (9 percent), Maryland (8 percent), California ((8 percent), and Minnesota (6 percent). The top five counties with a high concentration of sub–Saharan African immigrants were Harris County Texas, Bronx County, NY, Montgomery, MD, Prince George's County, and Hennepin County, MN. These counties account for about 15 percent of the total sub-Saharan African immigrants in the United States (U.S. Census, 2019).

New York and Washington DC metropolitan areas were the cities with the largest numbers of sub-Saharan African immigrants by 2017, followed by Minneapolis and Atlanta. These cities were home to about 36 percent of sub-Saharan Africans in the United States.

According to the Department of Homeland Security (DHS), in 2017 immigrant status who spoke English at home was 26 percent compared to 27 percent who reported limited English proficiency. It is no surprise about the higher level of proficiency because most sub-Saharan African immigrants come from countries where English is the official language. Other top languages spoken by sub-Saharan immigrants are Amharic, Somali, Beja, or other French and Swahili.

Education, Age, and Employment Among sub-Saharan African Immigrants

Sub-Saharan African immigrants are younger than their overall U.S. foreign-born population but older than the native-born. In 2017, 82 percent of sub-Saharan immigrants were of working age (18-64 years old), compared to 79 percent and 59 percent of the overall foreign-born and U.S.-born population, respectively. Sub-Saharan immigrants have higher educational attainment compared with immigrants overall and native U, S. citizens. In 2017, 40 percent of sub-Saharan Africans ages 25 and over held a bachelor's degree or higher compared to 31 percent of the total foreign-born population and 32 percent of the U.S.-born population.

Nigerians and South African immigrants were the most highly educated Africans with 61 percent and 58 percent holding at least a bachelor's degree. Others are as follows: Kenyans (50 percent), Ghanaians (39 percent), Liberia (31 percent), Ethiopia (30 percent), and Somali has the lowest educational attainment with 15 percent having graduated from a two-year college.

Sub-Saharan African immigrants also participate in the labor force at a higher rate than the overall immigrant population. In 2017 about 27 percent of sub-Saharan African immigrants 9 to 16 and over were in the labor force, compared to 66 percent of foreign and 62 percent of native-born adults (DHS, 2017). In addition, sub-Saharan African immigrants are more likely to be employed in management, business, science, construction, and arts occupation, than immigrants from other countries (Estrada & Batalova, 2019).

Naturalization

In 2017, 53 percent of sub-Saharan African immigrants were naturalized compared to 49 percent of all immigrants. Ethiopians were (60 percent), and South Africans were (59 percent), however, South Africans were more likely to be U.S. citizens. Sub-Saharan African immigrants were more likely than immigrants overall to have entered since 2000. About 70 percent arrived in 2000 or later compared to 47 percent of all immigrants (U.S. Citizen and Immigration Services 2019).

The Deferred Action for Childhood Arrival (DACA) program provides a reprieve from deportation and work authorization to qualified unauthorized immigrants who came to the United States as immigrants. As of April 2019, approximately 669,080 were active participants who benefited from the reprieve.

About 95 percent of DACA recipients were from Latin America or the Caribbeans, while those from sub-Saharan African countries were 0.5 percent of 3160 participants. Approximately 4.3 million sub-Saharan diasporans resided in the U.S. in 2017. This estimate includes individuals who were either born in the region or who reported sub-Saharan African ancestry (Estrada & Batalova, 2017).

Remittances

Those who have achieved the American Dream from Sub-Saharan Africa often send money to their home countries to support families and social programs. This is their way of giving back to the society. The number of remittances received by sub-Saharan African countries via former channels has increased exponentially since 2000, reaching $45.7 billion in 2018 according to World Bank. Global remittances accounted for about 3 percent of overall gross domestic products (GDP) in the region.

Some African countries economies have been more dependent on remittances than others. Remittance accounts for 15 percent of GDP in the Gambia and Lesotho and 12 percent in Cabo Verde and Liberia. Nigeria received by far the largest number of remittances in the region in 2018 for $24.3 billion. The money transfer accounted for 6 percent of GNP (World Bank Proposal Group 2018).

Part Two
Chapter Nine

A reflection on issues of importance towards the dream

The journey and beyond opens up discussions and examination of pertinent issues related to creating an environment to sustain the pursuit of American dream. These issues resonate with me, because we need to find the best alternative approaches with positive outcomes. Our civic responsibility reminds us that we can't be complacent about the needs of others simply because we have achieved our dreams, and therefore go to sleep. As concerned citizens, we need to get involved and let our voices be heard to bring about positive change. One of the benefits of education is to identify problems and be part of the solution. Here are the facts inherent in these issues.

It is known that the United States is the most powerful country in the world. America has done a good job in building both economic and military power, which other countries try to emulate. Many who have the opportunity would like to come to the United States to work and live in the country as permanent citizens. However, every country has its strengths and weaknesses. The United States is at a crossroads, in need of attention to maintain its position of power and prestige, as well as build a formidable future for its citizens to keep the American dream attainable for all.

According to the Heritage foundation, it is important to address issues facing the United States of America, to find solutions. To have more focus on these issues, one needs to ask this question – what type of America do I want to live in, work in, and raise my children in? The answer is obvious. I want to live in America where we work together to make the country better than what we inherited. This can be achieved by working together to promote productive ideals and discourage destructive behavior which undermine sustainability of the American dream. In this chapter, we examine some issues in our country that demand attention and review – namely, immigration, gun violence, drug abuse, and the state of marriage.

How Americans feel about immigration

A Gallop poll in 2019 found that 76 percent of Americans consider immigration a good thing for the United States. This is why we interject with our views on immigration policies and reform. As many as 81 percent support the idea of granting citizenship to undocumented immigrants on the condition that they meet certain requirements. Over the past two decades, congress has debated immigration reform policies. The following issues constitute the focus of the immigration debate: how to deal with the demand for high and low-skilled labor, the legal status of millions of undocumented immigrants living in the country, border security, and enforcement (CMS, 2017).

Finding a common ground on these issues has been elusive, so the debate continues, and a consensus is needed. The last time legislation came close to significant immigration reform was in 2013, when the Democratic-led Senate passed a comprehensive reform bill that provided a path to citizenship for undocumented immigrants and tough border security provisions.

However, the bill didn't receive a vote in the Republican-controlled House of Representatives.

Standing on the shoulders of early immigrants

Achievement of the American dream would not be possible without the amazing sacrifice of generations of early immigrants who arrived from every corner of the globe. By reflecting on their contributions, we are encouraged to join in the efforts to build a sustainable and formidable economy that would allow the United States to remain on top of the game globally. Immigrants over the years have played vital roles in crafting a nation known as the best in military power with the highest standard of living.

Succinctly, immigration creates prosperity in America and positions the country to lead the world in the 21st century. American immigration policy produces benefits and values. No other nation in the world welcomes new arrivals into its territory. Immigrants are contributors to the renewal of America's innovative capabilities and enable the country to excel in science and technology. America's solid economic ground could be attributed to efforts by immigrants in myriad ways:

Immigrants start businesses in the United States: According to the Small Business Administration, immigrants are more likely to start a business in the United States than native-born and make up 18 percent of owners of small businesses in the United States. **Immigrant-owned businesses create jobs for American workers**: According to the Fiscal Policy Institute, small businesses owned by immigrants employed an estimated 4.7 million people in 2007, and the latest report is that small businesses owned by immigrants generated more than $477 billion annually. **Immigrants are more likely to create jobs for themselves:** Report by the U.S. Department of Labor reported that 7.5 percent of foreign-born are self-employed compared to 6.6 percent among native-born.

Immigrants develop cutting-edge technology and companies: According to the National Venture Capital Association, immigrants have started 25 percent of public U.S. companies that were backed by venture capital investors among which include – Google, eBay, Yahoo, and Intel.

Immigrants are among our engineers, scientists, and innovators: According to Census Bureau, even though immigrants make up only 16 percent of the resident population holding bachelor's degree or higher, immigrants represent 33 percent of engineers, 27 percent of mathematical statisticians, and computer scientists and 24 percent of physical scientists. In addition, according to the partnership for a new American Economy, in 2011 foreign-born investors were credited with contributing to more than 75 percent of patents issued to the top 10 patents producing universities.

Immigration boosts earnings for American workers: It is known that increased immigration to the United States has increased the earning power of American workers with more than a higher school degree. Between 1990 and 2004, increased immigration was correlated with increased earnings of Americans by 0.7 percent and is expected to contribute to an increase of 1.8 percent over the long term according to a study by the University of California.

Immigrants boost demand for local consumer goods: The Immigration Policy Center estimates that purchasing power of Latinos and Asians – many of whom are foreign-born – will reach $1.5 trillion and 477.5 billion respectively.

Immigration Reform Legislation like the DREAM Act reduces the Deficit: According to the nonpartisan congressional Budget Office, under the 2010 House-passed version of the DREAM Act, the federal deficit would be reduced by $2.2 billion over 10 years because of increased tax revenue.

Comprehensive immigration reform would create jobs: Comprehensive immigration reform could support and create 900,000 new jobs within three years of reform from an increase in consumer spending, according to the Center for American Progress.

Comprehensive Immigration Reform would increase America's GDP: The nonpartisan Congressional Budget Office found that even under low investment, congressional immigration reform would increase GDP by between 0.8 percent and 1.3 percent from 2012 to 2016. These statistics have been provided to illustrate the relevance of supporting legal immigration initiatives for a stronger and more prosperous United States.

Gun Violence in the United States

As a concerned citizen, I take issue with unabated shootings, which cut short the lives of innocent people and deny them the opportunity to experience the American dream. The rate at which people are shot to death in the United States is alarming, unbelievable, shocking, and frightening, and the end is not in sight. It is a problem for all of us because of the number of mass shootings in public places. Mass shootings have taken place in various settings: churches, schools, restaurants, beauty shops, grocery stores, you name it. Gun violence is limitless; it occurs on the street, in homes, at workplaces, even in drive-by shootings on the highways.

Something has to be done to address this nightmare; it's like we are at war with ourselves. Living the American dream makes sense when all of us live in a nation where we work together, respect each other, and help each other, knowing that we are free to go about our business without fear of being shot down unexpectedly. In this section, we shall examine the nature of gun violence, what has been done by law enforcement, and suggested strategies to deal with the problem.

Available data from recent research for 2021 by the National Center for Health Statistics reported 38,390 deaths by firearm, of which 24,432 were from suicide, and 13,958 were by homicide (Howard, 2018). The rate of firearm death in 1999 was 10.3 per 100,000 persons, and in 2002 it was 12 per 100,000. This translates to 109 people dying every day by firearms. These statistics reveal the magnitude of gun violence. We have to deal with it.

About 1.4 million people have died from gun violence in the United States from 1962 to 2011 (Cook, 1997). To be more specific, this includes all deaths resulting from a firearm, including suicides, homicides, accidents, and mass shootings. In firearm deaths, compared with other developed countries, the United States ranked number one, and the Netherlands ranked lowest. The US death rate is 25 times more than most developed countries.

These statistical data are cited to bring to our attention the seriousness of the loss of lives from gun violence. This is why the ownership and regulation of guns are widely debated in the country. School shootings have become common enough that schools have drills where teacher and students practice how to huddle in silence to hide from imaginary gunman (Woodrow, 2018). Attempts have been made to curb gun violence from the federal level to the states, but gun violence continues to escalate. Other approaches implemented to address gun violence include restricting fireman purchases by youth, stiff sentences for offenders, and gun violence education for parents, children, and the community through outreach programs.

Gun availability. In 1997, there were 44 million gun owners in the United States. These owners possessed about 192 million firearms, of which about 65 million were handguns (Cook, 1997). Even though people claim gun ownership for protection and safety, it is not clear if that is true. The effectiveness of guns for safety and protection is still debated. It is known that the state with the most gun has the highest rate of gun homicide. In addition, higher gun ownership is positively associated with higher gun violence death. Other studies suggest that the concept of a gun can prime aggressive thought and aggressive behavior (Hepburn, 2004).

Mass Shooting. Mass shootings are incidents involving multiple victims of firearm-related violence, in the same location at roughly the same time. Eleven people were killed at Columbian high school in Colorado, seventeen people killed at Majority Stoneman, Douglas High school in Florida, twelve people were shot to death at a bar hosting a student party in California, and eleven people were killed when a gunman opened fire at the tree of life synagogue in Pittsburg in Pennsylvania. Four dead at Mercy Hospital in Chicago, three dead at a video game place in Florida, eight killed at the Spa in Atlanta Georgia, and ten people shot at King Sooper Grocery store in Boulder Colorado. There are too many of these incidents to mention.

Because mass shootings are sporadic it makes them too hard to prevent. Most mass shooters never commit a previous act of violence which makes it difficult to write a law to prevent mass shootings (Hepburn, 2017). The shooters have a common profile: alienated, disturbed, angry, and mentally ill. Mass shooters take time to plan the attack and the act is motivated by hate. Regardless of the rationale for the act of mass shooting, this hideous behavior must stop and must not be tolerated anymore. There are many good people who are fervently working to strategize workable solutions.

Preventing mass shooting gun violence. The Director of the Center for the Prevention of Violence Research has spent his life studying the effects of violence after seeing countless patients in the emergency room. According to the director, one of the primary ways mass shootings can be prevented is through an enhanced background check for gun ownership, although many states don't have a strict background (Stewart, 2019).

The director adds that he has seen gun sales at gun shows, where transactions took place in less than one minute without any background check. Some states have background checks in place but they don't monitor them (Stewart, 2019). A case in point, the director drew our attention to how automobile crashes killed several individuals in the 1950s, but as a result of research–driving regulations, and social changes, motor vehicle-related mortality declined significantly. He added that science played a role in the decline. "We can use scientific data to inform public policy, which can reduce rates of violence. I am sure we can accomplish this; we just need the opportunity to do this," he noted.

An added layer of gun violence legislation is called an extra risk restricting order. With this, the courts order allows firearms seized from an individual in crisis, or the order can be used to prevent firearm purchases. California was one of the states in the country to adopt this particular legitimation. They were potential mass shooting In California that was thwarted as a result of gun violence restricting order (Stewart, 2019).

Multiple polls suggest that a vast number of American support new gun policies. According to the National Survey of Gun Policy conducted in 2017, by John Hopkins Center for Gun Policy Research, about 87 percent of gun owners support gun violence restricting order. The director noted that mass shootings are challenging the character of public policing in the United States and creating an unprecedented action to preserve our fundamental right to safety in a free society. Finally, he noted that there are scientifically proven steps we can take to stop gun violence.

Domestic gun violence. An average of 760 people per year are killed by their husbands, wives, and dating partners according to an Associated Press analysis (Beckett, 2017). Most of the victims are women, wives, and girlfriends of the shooter. Sometimes the violence is murder-suicide, in which both partners end their lives. Laws that target domestic abusers have been found to have a moderate effect. Research studies found that laws restricting gun possession to violet abusers led to a decrease in domestic gun violence.

Suicide. Two-thirds of annual gun deaths in the United States – about 20,000 – are by suicide and states where gun ownership is higher is known to have a high suicide rate from gun-related death. It is known that suicide can be an impulse act and the availability of a gun in the moment of crisis could result in death with a gun. To stop suicide, the gun shop strategy is to use a friend of those contemplating suicide to intervene and take the gun away for some time until they calm down before giving the gun back to them.

What can be done about gun violence? When a mass shooting occurs, ideas float around about what needs to be done to prevent another one. But within weeks and months, life returns to normal, and people go about their business until another mass shooting takes place. There needs to be a fresh approach to stop the gun violence epidemic.

Some proposals come close to answering the question but stop short of a comprehensive solution. Let's take a look at some of them.

1. Banning military assault weapons might save lives but is unlikely to make a significant difference. Research studies reveal that America's gun violence problem is much bigger than mass shootings in which the victims are a tiny portion of overall gun violence death each year. The problem stems from favoring the irresponsible use of a gun over dealing with the issue peacefully, as is the case in several countries, particularly in developing countries.

2. Another approach is to focus on the small number of individuals who are at risk who use a gun to harm others and themselves (Beckett, 2016).

3. Experts suggest a ban on high-capacity magazine guns and rifles to limit the number of rounds they can fire. The shooting in Orlando shows that it is not what the gun looks like, it is how many rounds it can fire before reloading.

4. Cities that have done in-depth studies on gun control problems found surprising facts. The majority of the problem is driven by a small number of young men. Much of the violence is started by turf wars, for the most part by long-running arguments. Part of the solution is to initiate communication directly with these groups, offer assistance to help resolve the issues, and follow with better relations with law enforcement. This approach led to an immediate drop in gun violence in several cities (Beckett, 2917).

Drug epidemic in the United States

As noted earlier, the discussion on these issues is intended to suggest that behaviors identified as major concerns would make it difficult to achieve the American dream. Having lived in the United States for over four decades, I feel compelled to address issues in need of attention, to create more awareness and jointly work towards solutions. Everyone deserves to pursue and enjoy the American dream.

The increase in drug abuse in the United State is unprecedented. In 2013, an estimated 24.6 million Americans aged 12 and older had used an illicit drug. The number is up by 8.3 percent from 2003. Recent studies reveal the serious problem of drug usage and drug abuse. The age group most likely to get trapped are those between the ages of 18 and 25. About 70 percent of users who try the illicit drug at the age of 13 develop a substance abuse disorder.

Why do people use drugs?

There are many reasons why people use drugs, and continuous usage leads to addiction. The discussion of why people use drug is pertinent to expose the root cause of addiction, as well as understand the most effective approach to treat addicts and initiate preventative measures to stop addiction. Although legal drugs such as nicotine and alcohol are loosely regulated to stop minors from having access to them, an estimated 88,000 people die from alcohol-related diseases annually. Alcohol is the third preventable leading cause of death in the United States (Azate, 2018).

Some people who use prescription drugs may become addicted because they have access to the drugs, and believe it is safe to take since the doctor authorized it. Other people may use it to self-medicate, deal with depression, anxiety, stress, control anger, and feel happy. Drugs may temporarily alleviate bad moods, but unfortunately, as soon as the drug effect wears off, they become even more depressed (Azate, 2018).

Peer pressure plays an enormous role to influence people to try drug use. Peer pressure causes people to change their minds: to act irrationally, to do things to impress their friends and feel like they belong. Most teenagers start to use drugs with their friends not because they crave them but just to fit in.

Availability of drugs can lead to addiction, and frequent trips to the liquor store to buy alcohol could lead to drug dependency. Self-medicating is the top rationale for addiction. This is the case in which people use drugs to avoid depression, stress, loneliness trauma, anger, and pain, to temporality escape from reality.

As we now know why people abuse drugs, such causes could be treated. Drug addiction is treatable, and victims could regain their lives. Intervention programs are aimed to stop behaviors and practices which lead to drug abuse habits (Azate, 2018). Drug treatment help the person to stop using the drug, stay drug-free, and be a productive member of the family, at work, and in society.

Many options have been successful in treating drug addiction, including behavioral counseling. Counseling and other behavioral therapies are the most commonly used forms of treatment. Constant supervision and monitoring of people recovering from drug addiction are highly recommended to prevent relapses.

Social effects of drugs on society. According to DrugRehab.org, and Alcohol Abuse center, it is estimated that substance abuse rakes up an annual amount of $600 billion in the United States. Substance abuse imposes huge expenditure on the government, diverting money intended for other beneficial projects.

Other ripple effects of drug abuse include sexual assault, prison sentences, broken homes, child abuse, foster care placements of children from addicted parents, and work-related injuries. Every year substance abuse costs the health \care industry an estimated $180 billion, because healthcare is in charge of rehabilitation programs, mental disorders, and injuries related to drug abuse and alcohol addiction (Azate, 2018)

Drug abuse takes an extensive toll on the family which invariably cast a negative impact on society. Research studies show that a drug addict in the family could put a financial strain on the family budget – in other words, money for necessities could be wasted on recovery costs (Azate, 2018). Children of addicted parents receive less attention and are subject to anxiety, depression, stress, and violence. This leads to poor childhood health, reduces academic performance, and lack of interest in education.

Children of addicted parents are denied the necessities of parenting, and their contribution to society is hindered. In most cases, the emotional damage could lead their children to turn to t drug to escape from the pain exerted by years of neglect. In sum drug abuse is destructive to the victim, family, and society, this is why treatment is critical, because abusive habits could be treated, and everyone involved becomes a winner.

Drug use among young people

The reality is that drug abuse is a terrible disease and each individual that is addicted needs help. Throughout the nation, 10 million young people aged 12-19 need substance abuse treatment. People who begin using addictive drug substances between the ages of 13 and 15 are 7 times more likely to develop drug addiction (Yolkow, 2016). This is why it is critically important to keep young people away from experimenting with drugs before they get hooked and destroy their lives through addiction. Research studies indicate that for every year substance abuse is delayed during the period of brain development, the risk of addiction and substance abuse decreases.

Help for victims of drug abuse. The opportunity to help is all across the United States. People in all kinds of professions are getting addicted. There is a huge need for qualified counselors who can help people addicted to the drug. With the availability of qualified counselors, there is always a noticeable increase in the number of recovery cases.

Efforts to combat prescription drug overdose and addiction.
Communities over the United States have been devastated by increasing abuse and addiction over the last 15 years (Yolkow, 2017). According to Substance Abuse and Mental Health Services (SAMHSA), 11 million Americans misused prescription opioid

drugs in 2016. Nearly 1 million misused heroin and 2.1 million had an opioid use disorder due to availability by prescription.

Studies reveal a continuous increase in overdose death involving potent synthetic drugs which have claimed the lives of 300,000 Americans from overdose (Yolkow, 2017). In addition, preliminary data for 2016 indicated at least 64,000 drug death from overdose. This high death rate from overdose is heartbreaking and disturbing because too many of our citizens are losing their lives – robbing the nation of potential contributors.

In 2017, the department of Health and Human Services (HHS) outlined five strategies to provide the framework to leverage the expertise and resources of the agency in a coordinated manner to combat drug overdose:

1. Improve access to prevention, treatment, and recovery to enable addicts to achieve long-term recovery.
2. Target the availability and distribution of overdose drugs to cut off supply lines.
3. Support cutting-edge research which increases our understanding of addition to develop new treatment initiatives to reduce death.
4. Advance the practice of pain management to enable access to high-quality care that reduces pain for individuals and families going through treatment.

Creating awareness programs to stop drug use

The celebration of international awareness day is to remind all of us of the dangers of using drugs, and the consequences of its impact on human lives. The celebration highlights the destructive impact of drugs on individuals, families, and society. It is an opportunity to warn people of all ages to refrain from getting involved in drug use, especially young people who are at the age where peer pressure could result in experimenting with drugs.

Early use of the drug increases a person's chances of becoming addicted to drugs and could equally lead to drug overdose (Fowler& Yolkov, 2007). Since drug changes the structure of developing brains, so preventing early use of the drug is the best way to keep anyone from using drugs. National drug surveys indicate that some children start using drugs at the age of 12 or 13. Because the brain is still at the developmental stage, the drug has more chances of disrupting function in areas critical to motivation, memory, learning, judgment, and behavior (Fowler & Yolkow, 2007). In sum, prevention is the best approach to stopping drug use.

Awareness program. School-based awareness and prevention programs are directed toward young people likely to experiment with drugs. In addition, awareness and prevention programs are to prevent or delay the onset of substance use among young students. According to Rigg (2019), awareness and preventions are the significant effort of the National Strategy to reduce the prevalence of drug abuse. So, schools are pertinent settings for such intervention because drug use begins during adolescence. Schools provide easy access to reach lots of school children with prevention programs.

Facilitators. Facilitators lead the school-based programs by implementing a preventative-oriented curriculum with the students. The programs involve delivering classroom-based drug prevention lessons designed with interactive role-playing debates. Getting parents and the community involved during meetings where drug awareness programs are presented. Studies indicate that peer-led drug prevention programs are more effective than adult-led sessions (Riggs, 2019). The peer-programs are more effective because the effectiveness of the program is determined by several factors, such as the leader of the program. When the leader is a peer, member students are more interested in the prevention program (Cuipans, 2013).

Law enforcement. The police can make credible impact on drug awareness, and prevention programs because students are interested to hear from the police. The police enforce the law and knowledge to help the student avoid illegal substances. For example, students' perception of police is bolstered by the popularity of current television and movies that portray police work as thrilling and dangerous – always putting their lives on the line (Rigg, 2019).

International Narcotic Law enforcement. INL sponsors programs that demonstrated an increasingly effective reduction in drug use as well as drug crime. INL focuses on awareness efforts and prevention too -

1. To decrease and stop drug use
2. Delay the onset of drug use
3. Reduce the number of deaths from drug use

4. Reduce drug violence and criminal behavior

5. Establish self-structured drug prevention, treatment, education, and monitoring programs, in various parts of the world.

INL works with governments in 85 countries to implement drug awareness and prevention programs. In addition, INL assists countries, non-profit organizations, grass root organizations to form coalitions with countries in Latin America, Asia, and Africa. These initiatives have been effective to eliminate drug use.

Global Solution. Awareness and prevention of drug problems require intentional attention and action. INL collaborates with international associations such as the United Nations Office on Drugs and Crime (UNODC), the Colombo Plan, the Organization of American States, and the African Union.

INL supports a consortium of international interconnected organizations in the form of a new global association, for drug prevention and treatment. In addition, INL supports research-based prevention and treatment to identify and disseminate results aimed to reduce the demand for drugs. For example, INL research initiatives have been successful in targeting high risks youths, and women; the result has been effective in preventing drug use among these groups. INL remains committed to initiating novel approaches to prevent, reduce treat and consequently eradicate drug use.

In conclusion, it is patently evident that the devastating consequences of drug use are addiction disorder, overdose, and death. Drug additions affect all echelons of society and in every nation. Addicts include the rich, poor, educated, illiterate, men and women, as well as young people. Death from drug overdose runs in the millions and the trend remains unabated. Despite the toll drug takes on the body and lives, substance abuse hurts the economy and society.

Funds that could have been invested in beneficial projects are diverted into areas with no net return, such as going after distributors, drug-related crimes, preventative programs, and treatment. This chapter has been devoted to underscoring the problem emanating from drug use which should crystalize into an urgent, and more effective response to stop the flow of drugs in our nation as well as globally. We appreciate the ongoing efforts from the government, law enforcement, concerned organizations, and prevention and treatment establishments to save lives from drug-related deaths. The good news is that keeping away from drug usage increases the chances of achieving the American dream.

The state of marriage and family

We turn our attention to marriage and family as beneficiaries of this sacred institution. Most of us benefited from intact families and are conversant with the faith of others who unfortunately were raised in divorced homes, unwed mothers, or cohabitation homes. Part of the American dream is to support issues with relevance to ensure the continuity of our country- politically, militarily, and economically. Succinctly, evidence indicates that marriage is the bridge to prepare future generations, capable of sustaining our way of life.

There has been a sharp increase in the number of children who come from homes where the parents do not live as married couples. This trend has sparked vigorous debates among scholars, due to inherent family fragmentation (Daley & Wilson, 1985). According to the Institute for American Values, marriage has changed a great deal over the past two decades, with increased incidence of divorce, cohabitation, premarital sex, and unwed childbearing. Other pertinent changes include the dramatic increase in the number of working wives, reduced tolerance for domestic violence, and changes in gender roles.

Even though it is known that no marriage is perfect, support for marriage is based on the fact that numerous research studies conclude that marriage is an important social good, associated with impressively broad arrays of positive outcomes for children and their parents alike (Biblariz & Gottainer, 2000). Building good relationships matters and fathers are affected when they leave their families as a result of divorce.

Single mothers on average report more conflict and less monitoring when the father is absent than married mothers. In addition, adult children from intact family report being closer to their mothers than children from divorced parents (Acock & Demo, 1997).

In another study, 30 percent of young adults whose parents divorced reported poor relationships with their mothers, compared to 16 percent of children whose parents stayed married (Amato & Booth, 1994). On the other hand, fathers are at greater risk – 75 percent of young adults whose parents divorced had a poor relationship with their fathers. Succinctly,

127

divorce appears to hurt the relationship between the children and their father.

Cohabitation. Children from cohabitating unmarried parents have outcomes more similar to children from single mothers than children from intact families. Studies show that cohabitors have less income and lower education. Growing up in divorced homes affects the children. Children whose parents divorced or failed to get married are more likely to become young unwed parents, fail to get married, or have an unhappy marriage and relationship. Daughters raised from dysfunctional families are three times more likely to become unwed mothers than children from homes where the parents remain married and stayed together. Parental divorce significantly increases the odds that adult children will divorce and is likely to occur across the generation (Cherlin, 1995).

Marriage is a universal human institution. Marriage is acknowledged and celebrated in every human society. Since the beginning of recorded human history, anthropologists have documented the existence of marriage across all generations (Fisher, 1992). Marriage is significant in the reproduction of children, families, and society. While marriage may differ in various cultures, it is encouraged supported, and celebrated publicly across the universe.

Economic consideration. Economically, marriage can enable the couple to build wealth. Studies indicate that married couples build wealth faster than single or cohabiting couples. The economic advantage of marriage stems from two income sources as well as helping each other in times of need (Seltzer & Bianchi, 1988). Marriage couples build more wealth for the same reason that partnership, in general, is economically efficient. Married couples are more likely to buy homes that increase in value over time and may receive wealth transfers from both parents than couples who are cohabiting and not married.

Married men earn more than single men. Both in the United States and most developed countries, large bodies of research studies found that married men earn 10 percent to 40 percent more than single men (Hetherington & Kelly, 2002). The rationale for this disparity is that married men are more committed to their job, take up more responsibilities, are more disciplined, and tend to stay at the job longer than single men. Research studies indicate that married men tend to avoid substance abuse and arrive at their job on time. In addition, husbands benefit from the emotional support they receive from their wives and families (Hetherington & Kelly, 2002).

The negative impact of divorce. Studies show that divorce and unwed mothers bearing children cost the taxpayers over $110 billion, and the real victims are children. Divorce in a family has negative long-term consequences on children and impacts their socioeconomic progress. While children of divorced couples may not drop out of school, nonetheless as adults they have lower occupational status and have a higher rate of unemployment and economic hardship (Seltzer & Bianchi, 1988). Children from divorced parents are less likely to attend and graduate from college, as well as from four-year college. Children raised in single-family homes are likely to abuse drugs and alcohol, exhibit poor social behaviors, and commit violent crimes. Marriage remains a strong remedy to prevent children from developing onset bad habits.

Benefits of physical health and longevity in marriage. It is known that divorce and unmarried childbearing appear to have negative effects on children's physical health and life expectancy (Amato & Booth 1997). Longevity researchers suggest that parental divorce increases the incidence of health problems in children which continues into adulthood. Adults from intact families enjoy stronger health even in their old age.

In a research study conducted in Sweden – a country known for supporting single mothers with the nationalized healthcare system -- it was found that adults raised in single homes were more likely to report poor health conditions and die from them than adults raised in intact families (Amato & Booth, 1997).

In another study that followed a sample of academically gifted children for 70 years, it was found that parental divorce reduced a child's life expectancy by four years and negatively affects personality characteristics such as impulsiveness and emotional instability (Schwartz, 1995).

Another analysis found that older adults whose parents divorced when they were young were three times more likely to die earlier than older men whose parents stayed married. Research analyses suggest that the rationale for these findings is that parental divorce sets off a negative chain of events which contributes to a higher mortality risk among children from divorced homes (Schwartz, 1995).

Babies born to married couples have a lower rate of infant mortality than babies born from single mothers. On average, unmarried mothers with children run the risk of experiencing 50 percent of infant mortality than married mothers. Children born to unwed mothers have increased incidences of intentional and unintentional fatal injuries (Amato & Booth, 1997). In summary, marriage remains a powerful predictor of infant mortality, even in countries with naturalized health care systems and strong support for single mothers.

Statistics indicate that the rate of married couples continues to decline, which has consequences for our children's future, and the nation. It is known that families are indisputably the foundation of civilization. In addition, families are the sources of strong communities as well as ensuring the continuity of society.

According to Wood (2013), family breakdowns that impede normal family unity have been linked to poverty, and instability in the lives of children, which is problematic. Evidence indicates that marriage offers beneficial rewards such as financial success, emotional well-being, and good health for both parents, to raise children who are likely to become productive members of society.

Children from married couples are likely to experience higher academic performance, emotional maturity, and financial stability than children who don't have both parents in the home. Advocacy for marriage is based on its indispensability in sustaining the nation and provide the workforce needed for a better standard of living. (Wood, 2013).

Marriage is associated with less substance abuse. Married couples have a lower rate of alcohol consumption and less addiction to drug abuse than singles. Children whose parents stay married have a lower rate of drug and alcohol abuse. In the same manner, teens whose parents stay married have a lower rate of substance abuse and are less likely to experiment with marijuana, tobacco, and alcohol (Fleweling & Bewman, 1990). On the other hand, data from National Household Survey on Drug Abuse show that teens from divorced parents are likely to use drugs, alcohol, and tobacco as a coping mechanism.

Life expectancy for married couples. Figures from the Australian Bureau of Statistics show that the median age of unmarried adults who died was 52.2 years, while married adults died at a median age of 72.5 years (Fleweling & Bewman, 1990). Further studies revealed both men and women who stayed married had better health conditions and lived longer than divorced couples. Never married or divorced widows have a death rate that is 10.2 percent higher than married couples. Australian Institute of Health and Welfare report in 1994 revealed that divorced and unmarried men had a mortality rate twice that of married men. Overall, research studies found that being married has a positive impact on life expectancy.

Divorce appears to increase the suicide rate. According to research findings, divorced men and women are more than twice likely to commit suicide as married couples (Heath, 1996). In the last 50 years suicide rate for teens and young adults has tripled.

In recent studies, it was found that divorced men had a suicide level of 89 percent to 90 percent mortality rate than married men, while men who are widows had a higher mortality rate. In a research study conducted in Australia, it was found that the suicide rate among unmarried adults was three times that of married couples (Heath, 1996).

Married women have a lower rate of depression. Research studies revealed that married women have a lower rate of depression than unmarried and cohabiting mothers. Marriage is associated with aiding married women to cope with difficult situations which tends to lower their risk of depression (Heath, 1996). For example, in one national sample of 18 to 19-year-old single mothers, 41 percent reported having higher levels of depression, compared to 28 percent of married mothers in the same age group.

High depression level in single mothers has significant consequences for the welfare of infants. Depressed mothers are more likely to abuse their infants or abandon them out of frustration (Wilson and Daly, 1992). We have read in the papers or seen on the television about depressed single mothers who have hurt their babies and, later confessed that they were depressed when the action took place.

Some studies followed young adults as they got married, divorced, and lived as singles. Findings from such studies revealed that getting married and staying married boosts mental and physical health as well as emotional well-being for men and women (Heath, 1996). Further, a study by the University of Melbourne found that marriage generates greater life

133

satisfaction for both men and women. Researchers also found that being married contributes to 61 percent of the couple's state of satisfaction and happiness (Field, 1992).

Married women are less likely to experience domestic abuse. It is known that domestic abuse is prevalent and remains an issue of concern. However, research studies show that living with a man outside marriage is associated with an increased risk of domestic violence (Wilson & Daly, 1992).

Research analysis by the United States National Survey of Families and Households found cohabitors (meaning, in this case, couples living together but not married) were over three times more likely to experience domestic abuse. Cohabitors are more likely to report incidences of arguments, anger bursts, and fighting.

Summing up all of these research studies and analyses on why marriage matters, it is obvious that marriage is more than an emotional relationship, but rather a beneficial social good that has endured the test of time. It is pertinent to note that the decision to get married or not is a personal decision and in addition, not every child raised outside a married union is likely to succumb to failure and bad behaviors.

Nonetheless, the institution of marriage offers more benefits and better outcomes as discussed in this chapter for men, women, and children, than divorce, unwed childbearing, and cohabitation. As advocates for the protection of marriage, the recommendation is that policymakers consider providing funds for research studies aimed at fresh initiatives to strengthen marriage, which is good for children, families, communities, and the nation. It is our hope that parents work together to raise their children and provide them with necessary resources to enable them to pursue and achieve American dream.

Chapter Ten

Revisiting The American Dream

Being an American

In essence, to be an American is rooted in the U.S. Declaration of Independence, which h was created by the founding fathers. There are two key concepts that are responsible for shaping the dream. The declaration says that "all men are created equal." In other words, that each man/woman has the right to life, liberty, and pursuit of happiness.

The choice to become an American was based on my admiration of these articles which patently highlighted the importance and protection of human dignity, opportunity to pursue one's interests, freedom of choice and expression. Beside these privileges, another element that appealed to me was the structure of the government which allowed people to choose their leaders and, the power to express individual and group perspectives without retrieval.

Here is what President Franklin Roosevelt said about the American dream and being an American, on the occasion of the fifth anniversary of the Statue of Liberty in 1936. "They came to us speaking many tongues but a single language, the universal language of human aspiration. How well their hopes were justified is provided by the record of what they have achieved. They not only found freedom in the New World, but by their efforts and devotion they made the New World's freedom safer, richer, more far-reaching, and more capable of growth. We take satisfaction in the thought that those who have left their native land to join us may still retain their affection for somethings left behind – old customs, old language, old friends. Looking to the future, they wisely chose that their children shall live in the new language and in the custom of this new people. And these children realize their common destiny in America."

This speech summed up the ideals so many immigrants in the United States nurtured in their minds. The aspiration for everyone regardless of the country of origin is to live in a land where the environment is conducive to explore opportunities, develop initiates to attend success and contribute to make America an example of a nation where freedom, liberty, pursuit of happiness and unity are attainable. Most of the immigrants from the inception of this country have given back to America through enlistment in the military or participation in economic activities.

Since the inception of United States, immigrants have had common dreams and aspirations for coming to live in this land. In a letter written by J. Hector St. John de Crevecoeur in 1735 to his countrymen in England and Europe, he provided a glimpse of live in the new American colonies, expressing his affection as an American compared with what it was like living in Europe. He stated: "In this great American asylum, the poor of Europe have somehow met together in consequences of various cause." Two thirds of them had no country. As one early immigrant stated: "Can a wretch who wonders about, who works and starves, whose life is a continual sense of affliction or pinching penny. Can that man call England or United Kingdom his country? But here they come urged by a variety of motives. Everything has tended to degenerate them; new mode of living, a new social system; here they become men, but in Europe they were as so many useless plants. But like the transplantation of all other plants, their roots have taken and flourished. Formally, they were not numbered in any civil list of their country, except in those of the poor, here they rank as citizens." He went on to express his satisfaction and admiration with the new country: "By what invisible power has this surprising metamorphosis been performed?"

He then provides a clue about the role of government in the life of the people and the economy. "By the law and industry, the law protects them as they arrive standing at the symbol of adoption. They receive ample reward for their labor. These accumulated rewards procure them land and those lands confer on them the title of freemen. This is the great chain that link us all." This letter sums up the collective perspectives and expectation of what the American dream holds for immigrants and all Americans.

The American dream, in my perspective, is about living in a land where I am free to pursue my interest, and become successful, live a comfortable life with my family as well as give back to my community and the United States of America. Along the way, there are other ideas on what the American dream represents, but in the end, it is about the human propensity to live a free and happy life, coupled with hard work to pursue one's interest to the best of his or her own ability. In *A Brief History of the American Dream*, Sarah Churchwell (2021) noted that the phrase "American dream" is associated with upward mobility and enough economic success to live a comfortable life. On the other hand, the American dream reflects the idealism of the great American experiment which continue to evolve.

According to the Oxford English dictionary, the American dream is defined as "the ideal that every citizen of the United Sates should have an equal opportunity to achieve success and prosperity through hard work, determination and initiative." Other definitions, such as that of the American historian James Truslow Adams, deviate somewhat from this.

Adam distinguished the American dream from less focus on prosperity when he declared "not a dream of motor cars and high wages mainly, but a dream of social order in which they are innately capable and be recognized by others for what they are regardless of fortuitous circumstances of birth and position. In addition, the dream is about collective moral character, a vision of common well-being that is held in common and therefore mutually supported. In retrospect the dream is inclusive of the well-being of our fellow citizen at the end of the spectrum."

The origin of the American Dream

Before we delve into the future of the United States, it is pertinent to understand how the idea of American dream originated as well as current perspectives about the reality of the dream.

Prior to my arrival into the United States, the phrase "American dream" was familiar. I read about it in a variety of books, magazines, and news outlets. It reflected a lifestyle of freedom to pursue one's interest, create one's destiny, work hard to succeed and the opportunity to become successful in life.

The term "American dream" has become a household word; as such, it may be informative to trace its origin.

Literature review indicates that a historian James Truslow Adams received credit for being the first to popularize the idea of the American dream. Adam wrote a book in 1931 called *The Epic of America*, in which he expressed his idea thus "that dream of a land in which life should be better and richer and full for everyone with an opportunity for each according to their ability." However, the concept of American dream existed before Adam defined it. In 1630, John Winthrop gave a sermon to his fellow puritans titled "City on a Hill" as they sailed to Massachusetts. Although Winthrop never used the word "dream," he described his vision of a society in which everyone will have a chance to prosper as long as they all work together and follow biblical teaching. In other words, people should give each other the opportunity to contribute their special talents in a collaborative manner. The biblical principles pertain to being honest, peaceful, forgiving and sharing love for common good. Winthrop message resonated with the people in such a way it was accepted as a God inspired message – which encouraged the people to become united in their pursuit of collective and individual dreams.

The new mindset instigated by Winthrop's message to the puritans ushered in a new era in early American history. The attitude of the people became more positive, and they were ready to build a country like no other in the world. The notion that America is different from other countries evolved and grew throughout the 19th century. The United States became known as a land of unparallel opportunity where anyone could achieve anything if they dare to dream big enough.

Why is the American dream important?

The America dream is important because it offers hope and dignity to the human spirit, to attend to their highest potential towards success and happiness. It motivates individuals to live in freedom and pursue their interests entrenched in hard work, to become successful and live a comfortable live with their families. The American dream provides the bases for progress and unity and the encouragement for anyone to know that nothing is impossible to achieve with commitment and hard work.

American-dream idealism was instrumental in the establishment of the United States as a country when it broke away from Britain. In the Declaration of Independence, the American dream was an underlying theme with a link to freedom and equality of the people and was the impetus that overcame slavery in the 18th century. In addition, the phrase "American dream" touched on innate human desire to pursue individual aspirations based on one's capabilities. The abolitionists referenced to the ideals of American dream stating that equality and freedom were prerequisite for all American citizens.

The American dream has served as an inspirational reference source for all Americans who fight for their rights, and demanding attention in the society. For example, Martin Luther King referenced the phrase "that all men are equal" in his speech during the civil right movement. Dr. King believed that all people in the United States should be treated fairly, with the same equal rights and the same opportunities, just as it is stipulated in the Declaration of Independence. With such indomitable convention, King was able to mobilize many people of all races to support the movement, and in the end Civil Right Act was passed in the Congress for all American citizens. Since then, people are not afraid to fight for their rights on any issue that is important for various groups.

In terms of the economy, the American dream has promoted capitalistic ideology. The American dream exhorts capitalistic economic system, which is the catalyst for economic growth and development. Capitalism is cherished by proponents as an ideal system where each person is rewarded based on their efforts. Capitalism promotes hard work and underscores the importance of the rewards in form of better pay, advancement, and accumulation of wealth. The United States is assumed to have utilized the American dream concept, linked to capitalistic approach to successfully develop American cities.

The United States of America has experienced clear inequality and poverty even as more people pursue the American dream. These issues have triggered questions as to whether the American dream is for good or bad, since it ignores and instead promotes individualism and exhorts materialism in America. Having listed the positive sides of the American dream, we shall now go through issues that tint the ideals of the American dream toward negative polarity.

The downside of the American dream steams from the ambiguity of clarity in its interpretation. In reality, American dream proposes that each person has equal opportunities in the U.S. in spite of his or her background. This is not always the case, because many who are disadvantaged from the beginning, due to circumstances beyond their control, may fall short of high expectation as prosperity becomes illusive. The fact is that the majority of wealth is concentrated in the hands of the few wealthy individuals and the gap between the rich and the poor is widening in the nation. The dream could be considered unfavorable since it downplays the reality that U.S. is a land where power and wealth influence the outcome of issues.

The dream encourages individualism with a lack of concern for the poor members of the society. The dream promotes the attainment of personal achievement through hard work. Even though it is asserted that those who work hard have the opportunity to succeed, those who can't succeed are blamed for their problem. In the society, there are those who are set to live in luxury from wealthy backgrounds and others who have to struggle to make it, so the chance of achieving the American dream is not guaranteed.

Again, the American dream erroneously equates economic prosperity with happiness as well the ideals of creating a more successful lifestyle by working hard and earning more money, which is not the case. American dream suggests that once one achieves success – economic wealth and social mobility – that he or she will experience happiness., contentment, and satisfaction, which in reality is true to some and questionable to others. The dream exhorts materialism at all costs, and some would go to any extent to get rich with no regard to ethical conduct.

Arguably, the American dream is an ill-defined concept which has been stretched and adapted to accommodate diverse interpretations. This means American dream can be applied in different contexts both for noble causes and for selfish purposes. In summary, those who developed the phrase 'American dream" did so with good intentions because there have been significant positive outcomes.

Analyzing the dream

Although the United States is considered the richest country in the world, there are significant poverty and socioeconomic inequality. This is because the American dream could lead some to accumulate wealth to the extreme, since it is not restricted, and ignore the less fortunate. Over the years the dream has been redefined, to adapt to the changing times, nonetheless one thing that is certain in the dream is the emphasis on achieving prosperity, success, and living a happy good life.

The irony is that the dream is elusive to many, since individuals will always want more than they have which could result in a state of discontentment. Further, the dream mitigates social cohesion since it encourages individualism with overemphasis on material possession. The American dream is blamed for the promotion of capitalism which favors the minority who dominate ownership of businesses at the expense of the working class. On the other hand, capitalism has been practiced for decades in the United States with significant demonstrable economic success.

What it takes to live the American dream

Basically, the American dream is predicted in achieving one's dreams by utilizing innate capabilities to reach the highest level of success in a free society guided by the rule of law. Although individuals' dreams may slightly vary, the tenet of the idealism is encapsulated in achieving happiness. The article of independence elucidates patently the dream which many individuals from around the globe have identified with, such as the right to life, liberty, and pursuit of happiness. In this section we shall review what measures are in place to ensure that America remains a nation where dreams are nurtured with enough passion and determination.

Is the American dream still alive and well with immigrants?

The following questions in this chapter are asked to assist our understanding, regarding the rationale behind migration in the United States. What is the American dream to which immigrants are drawn? What is it that so many immigrants and undocumented immigrants are willing to leave their home countries and live permanently in the United States? How do immigrants fare while living in America?

A popular magazine in the early 1990s asserted that unemployment is low in Switzerland, owning a home is easier in Australia, attending college is affordable in Canada, yet dreams more often come true in America (Topolnicki, 1991). This statement underscores apparently why so many immigrants choose to leave their country.

By the end of the 20th century and the beginning of the 21st century, immigrants poured into the United States by the millions for the purpose of living a better life, earning higher income, acquiring homes, living better than their parents, and creating opportunities for their children. The desire to live a better life triggered massive immigration to the United States in millions from Europe. Asia, Central America, and South America. To early immigrants, achieving the American dream translated into having a steady job, a comfortable home, and a bright future for their children to succeed (Clark, 2002). Some immigrants who did well in their countries wanted to live in a place that offered limitless opportunities. In other words, it is that elusive search for improvement that is at the heart of the dream. In addition, the burning desire for upward mobility and to succeed were the forces behind the dream.

Dreams and the pathway to success. To achieve the American dream is considered synonymous with working hard to succeed. According to Hochschild (1995), the American dream is entrenched in achieving success – not only earning a high salary, a secured job, but the notion that even those who are poor with few skills can still succeed in an environment of limitless opportunities. As such, so many who are disadvantaged are optimistic about their future, knowing that there is a fair chance of becoming successful in any chosen endeavor.

The American dream has dual sides. On one hand, it is evidenced in specific defining symbols for example owning a house, a car, and arrays of consumer goods. On the other hand, the dream embodies both material possession as well as search for better life which is satisfying according to each person's ability (Clark, 2003).

Those who sought to interpret the American dream have suggested that it has always been more than the search for material possession, and evidence indicates that it actually goes beyond material well-being. However, recent criticism of the notion of American dream has focused on upward mobility and the idea that selfish and individual pursuit of the American dream only generates overproduction and the orgy of consumption.

Much of the current debate about the future of immigrants revolves around whether or not the path to social mobility is accessible to new immigrants. The questions to address these issues are: Do the new immigrants have a chance making it into the middle class and how many are making it? Will the one who arrived at the bottom remain at the bottom for how long?

Research studies indicate that progress has been made (Clark, 2003). Clearly a remarkable portion of immigrants have moved up into the middle class. Even though many are still behind, nonetheless having education and skills are important for upward mobility. Evidence indicate that over time immigrants move from the bottom to the middle class and have the resources to fulfil their dreams. House ownership among immigrants is rising but it is elusive for those at the bottom.

Preserving the American dream

We as a nation owe it to the future generation to inherit nothing less than the best country in the world, as strong as ever, both politically, economically, and militarily. Even though the America dream by subjective definition may not be perfect, it has motivated millions of citizens to attain to their highest potential manifested in unbelievable success and prosperity in the country. To preserve the dream, we need to close some gaps, and action has to be taken urgently.

There are two achievement gaps that need to be bridged, to keep the achievement alive for the future generation. According to Honda (2011), the first gap separates our communities by class and ethnicity. This could be divisive because it attacks the very principle upon which our nation was founded – a promise of equality, opportunity for all regardless of gender or race. Apparently, public school is the tool through which our society strives to deliver on the promise of equal opportunity. As such, when public education is replete with inequality, the foundation of our society becomes weak.

The second achievement gap is between the United States and other developed countries. It is palpable that the United States spends more per pupil than any other developed country, yet we compare poorly with other developed countries because our progress in reading, science and mathematics has remained stagnant in the last 30 years (Honda, 2011). Even though the spending is comparatively high, there is a funding gap outside the classroom. In consideration of all spending, the U.S. ranks dead last among developed countries.

With these statistics, it is not a surprise that the U.S. has the fourth highest child poverty rate among the developed nations. This is alarming because it amounts to weakening our competitiveness and security; in the global economy, education is the enabler of opportunity and the enhancer of long-term financial stability and prosperity. For the U.S. to remain a world leader in the 21st century, it has to ensure that our economy is competitive and built by the most skilled innovator and agile workforce (Honda, 2011).

The first achievement gap which separates our community by class and ethnicity threatens the authenticity of the American dream by denying each child equal access to realize his or her fullest potential. The second achievement gap represents an attack on the American dream itself because it threatens the viability of the middle class. According to (Honda, 2011), in order to address both of these gaps it is necessary to distinguish between equity and parity. For example, in California, while all schools are supposed to be established on the same standards, not all schools are treated equally.

Consequentially, any unfair statewide funding can harm low-income community students. To exacerbate the problem, the highest spending districts spends about ten times per student than the lowest spending district. Most of the better funded schools have high teacher salaries, lower teacher-student ratio, higher standardized test scores and higher graduation rates, than neighborhood districts which struggle with low funding. The poor and minority students often require additional resources to address needs that originate outside the classroom. By addressing the individual needs of each child regardless of the cost per pupil, equity can be attained.

Research findings indicate that the situation could be addressed successfully. For example, schoolteachers know which children are likely to drop out of school, they know where the achievement gaps exit, and given the tools, they can close them. Above all, the teachers know that the single commodity children bring to school each day is time and it needs to be filled with values (Honda, 2011).

To solve the problem of reforming school financing, and redefining the federal role in public education, Honda formed the National Commission on Education Equity and Excellence. He believes that it is by talking with teachers, parents, students, board members, counselors, principals, and superintendents that we can understand what is needed to make public education work in every community in the United States. According to Honda, we need to develop a new system of finance that empowers local community leaders to devise a unique approach that works for their community.

There is no single policy that will close the achievement gap for poor and minority students, but application of myriad of polices. When such polices are implemented, they will help to achieve our vision of equality for every child. The international achievement gap will close as all tools are employed to ensure that every child is successful. This approach will prepare our children to fully participate in the 21st century economy and beyond.

The state of the American Dream

The concept of American dream attracts attention because it encourages people to aim high and achieve their aspirations. Most individuals not only in America but elsewhere thirst to live a freer, more fulfilled life for themselves and their family. The American dream is so irresistibly appealing that millions of people from all over the globe are lured to the United Sates to actualize their dreams. A number of research studies have been conducted to determine how satisfied those who pursue the American dream are in their desire to achieve the dream.

At Xavier University in Cincinnati OH, American Dream Composite Index was established in 2011. This instrument was built to gauge people's perspectives on achieving the American dream. In addition, it measures the currents and collective sentiments regarding the extent to which people living in the United States are experiencing the dream. The drivers or aspirations of the dream include home ownership, carrier advancement, good education, and social status. Collectively, other unique aspirations include individual personal economic well-being, trust in the institution, attitude towards diversity and physical environment. The study found that the most important driver of the dream pointed to contentment, health, and prosperity in life (Smit & Fortin, 2014).

One of the interesting findings from the ADCI is that attitude towards diversity was rated too high. Participants responded positively to sentiment regarding their well-being. The research found out that, unfortunately, the dream of having a strong personal economy and a society where the people have trust in the institution received low approval. It was also reported that respondents admitted that they struggled with financial security, trust in the government and trust in business organizations.

Along these findings, respondents acknowledged that improvement in the areas of financial security, trust in the government and in business organization would improve the quality of life for Americans and enable more citizens to achieve their dreams. The American Dream Composite Index as of 2014 stands at 65.17 percent, which means that as a nation, we are 65.17 percent satisfied in our journey to fully achieve the American dream.

The good news is that the average AMDI score from 2011 until the present has increased each year. Overall quality of life in America is steadily improving, especially with the current economic expansion. But on the other hand, the overarching aspiration that have not been met yet includes the trust Americans have in government, which has regressed since mid-2012.

The trust people have in government stands at 38.74 percent, which means that Americans are only at 38.74 percent on their way to live in a society where the government can be fully trusted (Smith &Fortin, 2014). In comparison to government rating in other parts of the world, the rating is moderate, and there is plenty of rooms for improvement.

In short, the American dream is predicated on hope, in other words the hope that every individual of any status has the opportunity to reach their highest potential. On that note, hope is inextricably imbedded in our nation's ideals of freedom, equality, justice, and opportunity for all. Therefore, individual pursuit of the ideals intertwined with collective efforts constitute the moral and economic engine that nudges our nation forward.

In a survey conducted by ADCI, it was found that there is direct relationship between the number of individuals who pursue the American dream and the health of the society. There are many benefits when more citizens embrace the ideals of the American dream because it exhorts millions of Americans to pursue and actualize their dreams in a country known as the wealthiest nation in the world.

Guiding the American Dream for the Future

The American dream is worthy of preservation because it is functional. It is incapsulated in hope – for a brighter future for all. It must be guided with focus on elements that are relevant with enduring potentials. The purpose of choosing or designing our future is to establish the framework needed to focus our attention on relevant elements that would make a better American dream possible. Guiding our future in this narrative is about creating opportunities where anyone can participate and succeed.

Take, for example, our children. Some are from parents who have both the time and resources to invest in their children's development and live in neighborhoods with strong and cohesive social networks. They attend good schools and benefit from substantial public investments that exhorts and support them to succeed. On the other hand, some children are born into struggling families who face daily challenges that make it nearly impossible to take ideal care of the children. These families live in communities with unsafe environments, limited job options, and little chances of getting employed (Kirsch & Braum, 2007).

These communities have inadequate school and are shattered by poverty, as well as with constant violence. Based on differences in upbring, these children from unsimilar backgrounds apparently have different trajectories in their growth patterns, which creates advantages and disadvantages that ultimately influence the outcomes of their adult life. (NCCP,

2015). Research findings indicate that this polarization of life outcomes is not limited to any particular group; it is national in scope.

More than 16 million children, or 22 percent of all those under 18, live in families who have income below the federal poverty level (NCCP, 2015). About 13 percent of children are growing up in neighborhoods that are described as sometimes unsafe. More than one in five children were food insecure at some point in 2013, and about 13 million public school children were homeless at the start of 2012-2013 school year (CTDB, 2014). In view of this statistics, it is obvious that too many of our children are faced with tremendous barriers from birth, which would require heroic efforts to correct existing disparities, and create better opportunities for the children to succeed.

Palpably, this is the very antithesis of the American dream, which threatens not only the lives of individual Americans, but the very fabrics of our democratic society. Despite the hopes that accompanied national efforts such as the 1990s War on Poverty and the Civil Right Acts, and in spite of the progress that have been made, the current existing situation reminds us how further we need to go for all of us to actualize the American dream.

To effectively solve these problems of inequity and lack of opportunities the strategies to bridge these gaps must begin with and end with the children by improving parental care, expanding preschool program starting at ages 2 or 3 and helping parents to develop the skills needed to foster their children's social, emotional, and cognitive development. It is known that improving early childhood development is an important investment both for the children who are the recipients, and for the social and economic health of the country. Nonetheless, children's circumstances mirror those of their parents whose numbers are in tens of millions of adults, who need help and we can't afford to ignore them.

Here are the statistics we need to analyze to understand why action is urgently needed. Over 115 million adults in America are between the ages of 18 and 44. So many of them lack the education and skills they need to succeed in today's globally competitive technologically driven labor market (Kirsch & Baum, 2007). These parents need broader opportunities in order to improve their prospects for work, increase their abilities to earn decent wages, live in clean and healthy communities, with the kind of social networks and institutions that will support them and in turn improve their talents which they can pass along to their children (Kirsch & Baum, 2007). Ignoring these adults through lack of attention not only relegates them to a highly volatile future, but it also presents them with serious consequences for the children they are raising.

Early Intervention Needed

There is evidence that the accumulation of advantages and disadvantages experienced by one generation is increasing passed along to the next. As a result, life outcomes invariably relate to circumstances of birth. Consensus of opinions by Americans as a nation is that if we can't do anything, then we shall continue to drift apart, thereby placing an enormous strain on the country's social fabric which could reflect negatively on the characters of our democratic ideals.

By understanding these dynamics and transforming them into polices, we can improve equality of opportunity which is crucial not only for the individual outcomes and their children, but also for a stronger and united country. This narrative builds on dynamic elements of inequality and creating opportunities, with the goal of exploring and conveying them in a way to stimulates conversation on how we must urgently take action to ensure attainment of the American dream for all citizens.

Addendum to the American Dream

To achieve the American dream, the catchy phrase "it is not what you know that matters, but who you know" comes to mind. In view of today's technology-driven universe, it is apparent that it is what one knows that matters. To be rewarded generously the type of skills needed for employment and wages have become increasingly deep and broad. It is not enough just to know how to read, write, and to be a genus in solving mathematical problems. Organizations are more interested in those who can bring higher skills and the flexibility to adapt. Those who lack these skills may not fit in and may be struggling to grow in their carrier (Levy & Murnane, 2004).

In the United Sates today, equilibrium has shifted, with success depending on the ability to be nimble and acquire current relevant skills. The broad range in skills and knowledge that are necessary include interpersonal skills such as collaboration and teamwork, and character traits such as motivation, personality, reliability, and self-discipline. These skills are under the umbrella of human capital. In addition, success for now and in the future would demand other skills, which collectively are referred as social capital. Who you know incorporates the family you were born and raised, the social network that connects you with fellow members of organizations, teams, teams who provide support and advice, the social norms that guide one's behavior. Social capital serves to foster development and success (Putman, 2013)

Over the past two generations, social capital has become more strongly related to human capital. Inversely, those with human capital also tend to have networks, norms and behaviors that provide the most benefits in social and financial growth. The integration of human and social capital results in different lifestyles for the individual and their children.

In effect, the transmission of opportunities from one generation to the next comes with compounding advantages with one advantage leading to another advantage and equally one disadvantage leading to another disadvantage. The family in which an individual is born is increasingly influencing the degree of opportunity available to him or her in America today and the reality must be acknowledged that it is important in achieving the American dream.

Availability of Opportunity

In order to distribute opportunity equitably in America, two conditions must be met. A range of pathways must be open to everyone. Individuals must believe that they can make progress along those pathways if they invest in themselves (McCall, 2016). It is important to understand what opportunity means in this context, in order to actually take advantage of it. America is described as the land of opportunity and the American dream is predicated on it. Along this continuum, opportunity is present in situation or condition favorable for goal attainment. Opportunity can be defined as a pathway to engage in activities with rewarding benefits. To fully leverage existing opportunities, we need to eliminate gaps from human and social capital which contribute to widen inequality in life outcomes. If opportunities are to be more widely shared, we need to understand the forces driving access to opportunities.

Pathways that may provide access to opportunities include family structures, parental influence, financial resources, neighborhood, and community characteristics. Opportunities hinge on how individuals make choices about which pathway to pursue. Next, we shall look into human and social capital and the relationship to outcomes in the effort to achieve the American dream.

Relevance of skills

The high school certificate is no longer relevant to secure a ticket to the middle class. The relationship between education level and earning has changed in important ways over the last 50 years (David, 2014). There has been a clear growing advantage to male workers with college degrees. But unlike earlier eras, many alternative career paths involve the use of new technologies and as a result require more than high school education as well as specialized skills (Holzer, 2015).

The differential consequences in credentials and skills have impacted the current economic landscape, shaped by globalization and technology. There has been changes on how we communicate and access information due to digital networks. People are able to collaborate across borders and purchase goods at international marketplace. Over the past half-century, these forces have led to changes in our economy and unfortunately devastated the American economy and workforce.

Palpably, the skills required of many workers two generations ago, consisted of those with high school education. But now, there is a demand for higher skill due to a technology-driven economy, the rapid pace of change, and global completion that has rattled the workplace. Organizations are looking for those with technical and problem-solving skills, along with communication and collaboration. Employers are also seeking employees who have skills to be able to benefit from training programs and have the ability and initiative to learn and upgrade their skills on their own (and continuously).

The ability for workers to sustain good wages and increase opportunities for advancement in their careers depends entirely on the skill level they find themselves. There are three types of skill levels that we shall look into in this narrative. Low-skill workers are those with high school education or less. Middle- skill workers have more than high school education, but less than bachelor's degree (e.g., associate degree, post-secondary certificate), and high skill workers have bachelor's degree or higher (Goldin, & Katz, 2008).

Those with low skills in the U.S. have been hit hard as a result of increasing sophisticated technology. Millions of low-skill jobs have disappeared. For example, many assembly workers have been replaced by industrial robots, and self-service scanners are doing the work of cashiers. Other jobs have been exported to take advantage of low labor cost from developing countries. The loss of low labor skill manufacturing and production jobs has been offset by increase in low-skill service jobs such as food service, call centers and retail sales. For men with high school diploma, median earning decreased by between 1960 and 2013. The point here is that jobs don't pay enough to promote the economic and social stability of employee and their families. For families with low wages, two income earners are needed to take care of economic necessities of the family. Millions of individuals have two to three jobs to be able to meet their financial obligations. These low-skill employees struggle to survive because the jobs tend to be part time, some without benefits such as health benefits or sick leave, thereby putting workers at risk. With this scenario, missing a day of work due to illness not only reduces their income, but put them at risk of losing their jobs (Goldin & Katz, 2008)

For the middle-skill workers they have been impacted by the changing workplace as much as the low-skill workers. This is because technologies that excel at repetitive tasks involving storage, processing and retrieval of information continue to replace workers who perform repetitive work, including clerical work, meter reading telemarketers, and travel agents. Such jobs made up 58 percent of the jobs in the 1981; now they are at 44 percent (Cherenukhin, 2014).

Not all categories of middle-skill jobs are declining. Employment opportunities still exist in areas such as technical jobs in healthcare fields, radiation and therapist jobs, or installation, maintenance, and repair of mechanical/heavy vehicle systems. These jobs differ from the traditional middle-skill jobs because they involve the use of new technology training beyond high school education. Those who are able to complete the required training have good opportunities for employment (Chereremukhin, 2014). According to Robert Lerman, an economist, a robust apprenticeship system is one pathway that workers could develop occupational and employability skills needed to secure a job.

Decent-paying professional jobs exist for non-college educated individuals, but they require retraining young adults to acquire the skills needed for such jobs. In addition, we need to provide more work-based training in career-oriented fields as well as exhort apprenticeship with local firms. Based on current trends, U.S. has an underdeveloped apprenticeship system. However, private sector efforts are underway across the country to improve the situation (Goldin and Katz, 2008).

A report from a local staffing agency in the Houston area stated that 60 percent of job seekers were disqualified due to lack of skill for the jobs. Experts believe that the shortage in skilled workers is because local high school students were channeled towards four-year university degrees, instead of pursuing technical degrees. While there is no doubt that four-year college education pays dividend, it is helpful to have an alternative path to middle class.

In addition, variation among individuals and differences across regions of the country must be taken into consideration. Such differences are too great to take "one size fits all" approach to expanding opportunity. Rather, there should be a focus on identifying and supporting multiple pathways to develop the skills and knowledge needed for the jobs of today and in the future (Goldin & Katz, 2008).

High-skill workers

Job insecurity is not limited to any skill level, because the range of jobs displaced as a result of technological advance remains unabated (Brynjolfsson & McAfee, 2014). By combining computer power with more sophisticated software, it will be possible for a growing number of complex cognitive tasks to be automated. Invariably, technology can take on an ever-broadening set of jobs such as medical diagnosis, certain types of research, tutoring, accounting, and translating.

On the average, an individual's ability to find and keep a good job is related to the skills brought to that job and the growth potential which comes with practice over time. Better skills result in better economic outcomes which is a panacea to achieving the American dream. Advancement in technology, which has over the years has replaced the need for certain level of workers, should be addressed through skill development.

Bridging the skill gap to create opportunity

Although there is emphasis on the importance of skill development at the workplace, there is also important need to develop skills required for everyday life as a result of new technologies and changing business practices. For example, more and more tasks in our daily life require the ability of an individual to navigate, complete tasks, solve problems in today's data-intensive complex digital environment (Smith, 2012).

Even though there is growing expectation that everyone has access to a computer, internet, or smartphone, in reality not everyone is capable of navigating the online portal. It is true that computer access has dramatically increased as the digital divide continues to shrink, but the skills required to operate in the domain are often lacking. Those who don't have the skills are disadvantaged and left behind, and many are not employed for that lack of skill.

Research studies indicate that over 60 percent of adults in the U.S. scored in the lowest and most limited level of digital skills, below what is needed to evaluate, organize, and utilize the information from the digital environment. The importance of education attainment continues to receive attention from diverse groups, as a result there has been a national focus on increasing attainment rate to make sure that more students graduate from high school, and more students go to college.

The good news is that there has been improvement in high school graduation rate of 81 percent since the 2012-2013 school year. Similarly, the percentage of students enrolling in college increased by 46 percent from 1990-2014 (Smith, 2014). Myriad sources or pathways are available for anyone to acquire the skills necessary to improve their financial and social statues. By tapping into available opportunities, it becomes much more possible to achieve the American dream.

Chapter Eleven

Incorporating diversity to succeed

Nothing remains the same and change is inevitable (Ezidinma, 2021). America of the future is predicted to represent a nation of interracial citizens resulting from new immigrants and interracial marriages. The trend started years ago and will escalate as America's young people payless attention to racial segregation but rather embrace interracial dating and marriages. Among developed nations, the U.S. has more liberal policy towards immigrations, and as such, more people come to the country from virtually all over the globe to visit or reside permanently. This scenario contributes further to our diversity as a nation.

In this section we review pertinent aspect of our country's demographic makeup and how we can leverage our racial and ethnic differences for a better and more cohesive nation, to advance our founders ideals in creating a country where everyone is free to pursue their dreams to their best potential in the quest to achieve American dream. We shall also highlight the uniqueness of America's attitude to welcome immigrants from all over the globe to integrate into the society, and to contribute to make it better than they inherited it.

In the next four decades, the U.S. will rely on immigrants from different parts of the world to compete and develop uninterrupted. The U.S. will be reshaped and re-reenergized by an increased racial and ethnic majority (Kotkin, 2010). Based on this predication, demographic changes will affect U.S. relations with the rest of the world, and the U.S. will likely remain a unique multiracial superpower with formidable cultural ties with the rest of the world. America in the next four decades will look quite different from what it looks like in 2021.

By 2050, the vast majority of U.S. net population growth will come from ethnic minorities, especially Asians and Hispanics, including existing mixed-race population (Kotkin, 2010). By the middle of the 21st century, America will have no clear majority race. In 2010, 64 percent of the U.S. population was white but by 2050 it may be 50 percent minorities. Latino and Asian population is projected to triple, and because of that one in five Americans children will be Latino, and the population will continue to escalate.

The percentage of American's mixed-race marriages is growing exponentially among people under 18 years old. For example, in California and Nevada, mixed marriage rates are more than 13 percent, and in the Southwest, much of the Latino population is intermarrying with other ethnic groups. This trend is expected to increase in the future as the momentum remains unabated.

According to Teen Research Unlimited, 60 percent of American teens say they have friends from different ethnic background. In addition, Gallup Poll 2006 showed that 95 percent of young people (18-29) years old, approve of interracial dating, compared with 45 percent of those over the age of 64 years old. As Kotkin noted, Europe will continue to be a source of immigrants as many young Europeans continue to find their ways to United States.

However, the largest group of immigrants will come from Latin America, China, Africa, Asia, and other developing countries. The United Nations estimates that 2 million people will move to developed countries annually and more than half will come to the United States. If economic opportunities continue to show signs on positive outlook, more people will be motivated to migrate to the United States in pursuit of American dream, for themselves and their families.

Why U.S. is unique with diversity issues

In contrast to the burgeoning diversity population in the United States, some rival countries seem less able to embrace high level of interracial mixing based on their traditional insula culture. For example, China, Japan, and Korea are culturally resistant to diversity, and likely to frown on large-scale immigration even though much of the labor force is old and some go to work in wheelchairs (Backstories, 2019). Further, given Europeans current issue with immigrants, it has difficulty opening its borders to immigrants, and to complicate the issue, many Europeans are considering measures to curtail immigration to their countries significantly.

Diversity in the U.S. which primarily reflects the changing ethnic population, will play a pronounced leading role in the next national and global economic transition. A case in point, recent immigrants have shown remarkable entrepreneur talents - forming business startup level to the most sophisticated technology companies in the world. Between 1990 and the 200, immigrants started one quarter of all venture's companies in U.S. In addition, several American companies are increasingly led by people who came to America from different nations, including 14 of the CEOs in the 2007 Fortune 100. As Kotkin predicated, America in 2050 will seem to be like a foreign country. Our continuing racial evolution will still confirm the basic optimism of the society and its ability to adapt. In other words, our experiment to create what Walt Whitman in 1855 dubbed as the "race of races" will represent one of the greatest accomplishments of the mid-21st century America.

Dealing with diversity in the U.S.

Diversity in America is apparent and the rate at which it is increasing has generated both positive and negative responses. There are those who welcome it, embrace it, and celebrate it; and those who oppose it out of fear and try to avoid it. Those who go to the extreme to stop it become angry and hateful. According to LarBur (2021), such responses have direct impact on shaping political and social policies to deal with it in a way to highlight the benefits. It is important to understand that diversity allows for different groups to practice their cultural values, religion, cuisine, and language, without out fear of reprisal.

Diversity tolerance in essence "reflects the true America." To prepare for the shift we need to leverage our knowledge on how people feel about it, react to it and deal with it on personal and societal levels. A recent joint study from Princeton and Oxford University found that people can and do adapt to diversity as well as benefit from it (LarBur, 2021). This finding is critical for those in power to utilize it during policy formulation to integrate people and create a more cohesive society.

However, for those who are resistant to it, research findings revealed that they perceived diversity as an unwanted change in the definition of America. In reality, such insecurities are unwarranted, because research studies indicate that with time people can adapt and slowly start to see new benefits. It's known that even when people from different ethnic groups are given a chance to live together, it does not take too long for them to integrate. On the other hand, when people are pushed out or rejected, the outcome results in violence, disruption, or protest.

Tolerance to diversity is perceived as a norm (LarBur, 2021). Research from the University of Wisconsin found that showing people how their peers feel about diversity in their social circle increases their positive feeling about those with different backgrounds. In other words, when people observe that others around them share positive attitude about diversity, it increases diversity tolerance. Those exposed to diverse groups of people mixing together perceive diversity as a social norm and embrace diversity and get along with different groups.

Immigrants contributed to American culture and enhanced our influence in the World

Immigration issues continue to make headlines during and after presidential campaigns. Debates are held on issues concerning legal and illegal immigration. It was noted that Benjamin Franklin was concerned that too many German immigrants would change America's predominantly British culture. During the same period, a wave of new immigrants – the Poles, Italians, Russian Jews – were considered unlikely to assimilate into American life. The same fear was raised about Latin Americans, Asians, and Africans.

However, it turned out that immigrants enhanced the richness of the American society. The truth is that immigration is not undermining the American experience, rather it is an integral part of it (Griswold, 2002). Succinctly stated we are a nation of immigrants, and our different cultures, contribute to our strength. In other words, successive arrival of new immigrants has kept our country demographically young, added to our productive capability to become a major economic leader in the world.

Economic advantages. Immigrants contribute to position the United States as a major economic leader in the world. Immigrants bring innovative ideas and entrepreneurship spirit to boost the economy. As a result of immigration, business contacts are made with immigrants' home country, thereby stimulating demand for American-made products and technical assistance. According to a study by the National Academy of Sciences, immigration delivered a significant positive gain to the U.S. economy. As federal Reserve Chairman Alan Greenspan said: "I have always argued that this country has benefited immensely from the fact that we draw people from all over the world.."

In terms of the labor market, immigrants don't push American out of jobs — contrary to myths. The fact is that immigrants tend to fill jobs that Americans are reluctant to fill, mostly at the high and low end of the job market. Immigration results in increase for demands for goods and services as well as create employment opportunities for workers.

The contributions of immigrants are apparent in the high technology and other knowledge-based sectors. According to technology experts, Silicon Valley and other high technology sectors will cease to function if we permanently close our borders to skilled and educated immigrants. Immigrants represent human capital that makes our entire economy more productive. In addition, immigrants develop new products such as the Java computer language that has created opportunity for millions of Americans. Immigrants contribute to argument government finances rather than drain it. NAS study found that the typical immigrant and their household will pay a net $80,000 more in taxes during their lifetime, than they collect in government services.

Griswold (2002) argued that the flow of immigrants in recent times is not unusual even though opponents think that it is getting out of hands. Today about 10 percent of U.S. residents are foreign-born. The truth is that immigration can't be blamed for overpopulation. For instance, U.S. population growth of 1 percent is below the average rate of the last century. Realistically, without immigration our labor force would shrink with negative consequences on productivity. Based on the 2000 census, 22 percent of U.S. counties lost population between 1990 and 2000. Immigrants are needed to revitalize declining area in the country (Griswold, 2002).

Immigrants in the American workforce

Most immigrants enter the U.S.A. for the primary purpose of earning an income to better their standard of living. The workforce obviously comprises of American born citizens and immigrants from different parts of the world. The issue of workplace diversity deserves attention and needs to be discussed to derive the benefits immigrants bring to the work environment. In this section we shall discuss specific pertinent issues which could enhance immigrants' productivity in the workplace, in the quest to achieve the American dream.

Workplace diversity. Workplace diversity (WPD) relates to the differences that exists between people working together within a group in an organization. These differences need to be discussed to create an environment where there is improved communication, collaboration, and greater productivity. The complexity of WPD transcends the recruitment and treatment of workers in the workplace, but rather it has become one of the most challenging issues facing businesses and organizational management.

Efforts to improve WPD could yield dividends. Research studies reveal that workplace diversity under friendly environment enhances critical thinking, problem solving, and employee performance. Organizations with collaborative diverse workers attract talents, good will and enjoy competitive advantage as a result of collective brainpower. To derive the best benefits from workplace diversity, attention is given to challenging issues considered impediments to a successful workplace environment.

A critical Review of WPD. Proactive organizations are exploring strategies to exploit growing diversity of workers for competitive advantage. According to Pew Research Center the existence of a single or racial ethnic majority will cease to exist by the year 2055. Other studies estimated that over 20 million employed in the U.S.A. are immigrants. In addition, it noted that the U.S.A. and many developed countries will become pluralistic in the future (Emma, 2055). This paradigm shift in the global demographics is likely to morph into challenges and prospects in the workplace. Concerned organizations are actively integrating their initiatives into their recruiting processes to ensure that the best talents are hired from all over the world. Research studies indicated that the future workplace in the U.S.A. would experience apparent diversified workforce (Patrick & Hicks, 2012).

To derive maximum benefits from WPD, critical issues hampering those efforts need to be discussed. Adequate and successful analysis are likely to yield empowerment culture, build effective communication, team synergy, and increased productivity. Many organizations have embraced diversity to foster creativity, openness, innovation, and financial growth (Dike, 2013). Modern organizations are aware that diversity can be a critical link between corporate strength and overall performance (Christian & Moffit, 2006).

The benefits of diversity

As an immigrant with African heritage, I embraced diversity and it yielded dividends. I have workers from different ethnic and racial backgrounds. Through collaboration and contributions of fresh ideas we have more productivity and enjoyed competitive advantage resulting in more financial reward for each of us. No other nation in the world is as diversified as the United States. With diversity comes some inevitable challenges due to differences from ethnic backgrounds. However, for over two decades attempts have been made to deal with issues arising from racial differences, and regardless of ethnicity people have learned to tolerate each other. By moving past our differences, it becomes easier to tap into our commonalities and harness the power and befts of diversity. I have worked in organizations with diverse co-workers and experienced amazing results when people come together and focus on the job. Diversity in any setting could yield dividends like these:

Critical thinking and problem-solving skills. Well-managed diverse groups are likely to contribute and improve decision making through collective critical thinking. Employees from different backgrounds and cultures are likely to present varieties of perspectives towards challenging problems thereby creating opportunities to solve the problem. In addition, diverse employees can provide critical thinking in areas such as innovation, alternative solutions, improved operational strategies, money saving ideas and technological driven applications (Dike, 2013). Diversity allows for sharing of personal views, better relations, and respect for racial differences. Research studies reveal that well-managed diverse workforce could lead to elimination of biases, discrimination, prejudice, improved racial harmony as well as lessons in conflict management (Walia & Malik, 2015).

Employee growth and development. Exposure of employees in an environment of varied cultures, opinions and different backgrounds can stimulate personal growth, skill development and broad world view. Diversity enhances creativity, collective innovation, effective trouble shooting, and faster project execution. Employees in a diversified environment are likely to undertake challenging circumstances with successful outcomes (Walia & Malik 2015).

Unification of diverse strengths has the potential to create a positive corporate culture with high morale, greater output, and competitive advantage. Research studies indicate that cross-cultural understanding could stimulate better working relationship, better working environment, which is necessary to dispel stereotypes, prejudice, bias, misconceptions of people from different background.

Corporate Attractiveness. Workplace diversity is known to impact the attractiveness of an organization or associations. According to (Robinson & Dechant, 1997), companies that promote diversity and inclusion bolster their attractiveness to future employees and portray a positive image. In addition, organization could derive competitive advantage by encouraging diversified workforce with talents. Diversity in the workforce could stimulate novel ideas especially with millennials Gen Z (Emma, 2015).

Another research study by Esty & Hirsh (1995) reveals that workforce diversity enhances employees' satisfaction and positively improves conflict resolution as well as exchange of cultural information. Business contacts resulting in higher revenue and profitability have occurred in some organizations through immigrants in the U.S.A. (Robinson & Dechant, 1997). In the era of scarcity of skilled employees attracting best talents could enable companies to boost productivity, better margin, and accelerated growth.

Innovation Capabilities. To succeed in a fast-changing business environment, companies need to acquire the ability to adapt and evolve to compete through the introduction of innovative new product designs and quality services. Such initiative could be achieved through tapping into talents pools of a diverse, skilled workforce. Employees with different backgrounds often contribute different knowledge, experience and skills needed to nurture innovative ideas and critical thinking (Robinson & Dechant, 1007).

According to Hospers (2003), multilingual employees from variable sociocultural backgrounds could contribute to open new international markets through net-working contacts from their home countries. Research studies indicate that diverse group of employees outperform homogenous employees. The study highlighted that inclusive leadership could help companies maximize the benefits of diversity and, avoid the pitfalls of homogeneous workforce that stifles creativity and innovation (Hewlett, & Gonzales, 2013). Overall, adoption of diversity in the workplace is a prudent strategic decision which could translate into organizational capability to compete and succeed both domestically and in the international market arena.

Managing Workplace Diversity. Diversity is defined by differences in language, religion, gender, ethnicity, and nationality. Such differences could affect the way most immigrants are treated with negative attitude including hostility, discrimination, disrespect, and bias in the workplace environment. With the workplace increasingly comprised of individuals from different countries in the world, the issue of diversity is taking the center stage, highlighting both its relevance as a major competitive edge and the challenges inherent in it.

Proactive organizations have established polices in favor of diversity adoption, to leverage the benefits emanating from well-managed diverse workforce, and equally extricate impediments arising from workplace diversity. One of the challenges that requires attention about diversity in the workplace is on the issue of communication which could adversely impact work performance. Most immigrants are challenged with fluent communication and that could hinder advancement and success in the organization.

Communication in the workplace. Communication is an important tool which creates and maintains cohesion in discharging business processes (Hospers, 2003). Cohesion is crucial to the attainment of organizational goals, objectives, and completion of projects. Through fluid communication, the contribution of each individual could be harnessed for greater productivity, teamwork, informed decision making and organizational growth (Dike, 2013).

Inversely, poor communication can breed confusion, misunderstanding, lack of continuity, conflicts, mistakes, loss of

176

opportunities, less productivity, and dwindled margin for the organization. In addition, poor communication could result in missed deadlines, incorrect goal assumption, and low morale among employees. Workers with communication challenges could negatively impart collaboration and output (Patrick & Kramer, 2013). In light of the issues arising from poor communication, and other challenges, support for diversity in the workplace and in the society remain unabated. The need to derive the benefits of diversity has prompted training programs in several organizations.

Training programs. There are compelling reasons to expend resources toward diversity training in the workplace. Diversity offers organizations ample opportunities to compete and grow in the increasingly global marketplace. Various studies have shown that diversity management has positive impact on key aspects of organizational performance. According to the McKinney report, programs designed to address workplace diversity are effective and provide organizations with competitive advantage.

Chapter Twelve

Perspectives on America of the future

Since the inception of our country, the United States of America continues to morph politically, economically, and technologically, as well as developing in an unprecedented movement towards racial integration. Martin Luther King once said that American is an idea in development, and it turns out to be true based on available resources in human capital – intellectual prowess backed by financial resources to formulate and implemented strategic initiatives to remain the leader in both militarily and economic growth. The key to greatness in the United States is the power base which fuels growth for the futures. This power base is derived from the structure established in the immigration policy, importing the best talents from all over the world for collective productivity.

Challenges and barriers to reclaiming the American dream

To clear the way for individuals to actualize American dream, it is pertinent to dismantle barriers to this progress. In this section we shall extrapolate the factors essential to provide the platform towards brighter future for dreamers in the United States of America. This will include eradication of discrimination and bias, improvement on racial relationship, inclusiveness, minority participation, enforcement of anti-discrimination laws, and equal opportunity for all.

As a result of discrimination and racial bias in most cases many people have been shut out from the route to actualize American dream. According to Hecht (1959), as a country with racism in its history, racial opportunity gaps have been created and perpetuated by the public and private sectors. One of the most obvious pieces of evidence of this reality is the enduring legacy of redlining. Redlining refers to refusal to extend loans to minorities because they live in certain neighborhoods, thereby restricting their mobility into majority white neighborhood.

By refusing to allow minorities access to loans, the FHA kept minorities locked out of the opportunity to build wealth through house ownership. This unfair practice set a course for racial segregation that characterize most of the communities in the United States (Hecht, 1959). The disconnect resulting from insidious pattern of exclusion has led to inequality and lack of opportunity to achieve the American dream particularly for minorities and most immigrants. Attempt to correct the inequality has always represented an immense dilemma for the country. Advocates for equal opportunity for all are determined to go through the legal process to ensure equal opportunity for all which is promised to every American by the constitution.

From the inception of the United States, it has been a nation of immigrants. In 1970, according to the national census, the white race constituted 80% of the population (175 million) with the remaining 20% (27 million) comprising of minorities of different racial groups. Research studies indicate that the racial composition has been in continuous flux since the 1970s. By 2050, the United States will no longer have majority racial claim (Cohn & Caumont, 2016). For example, states such as California,

Texas, and Washington DC have population with minorities forming the majority. The racial composition of our country's population has been acknowledged and discussed for many years, but the economic implication of this shift is neither patently understood nor broadly accepted by most Americans (Hecht, 1959).

According to Brookings demographer William Frey, increased Hispanic and Asian immigrants, combined with a rapidly growing multiracial population, has enabled U.S. population to grow despite a shrinking white population. This diversity explosion is what has enabled the United States to avoid the plight of other developed countries in Europe and Asia, who face diminishing workforce. Low birth rate and little immigration have led to concerns about the implication of an aging workforce. Currently, in Asia and Europe there is insufficient number of young adults to replace older workers when they retire.

Creating opportunities for minorities and immigrants to achieve American dream is pertinent to ensure brighter economic future for the country – especially where we rely on a consumption-based economy for business growth and availability of job opportunities. The existence of unequal opportunity would obviously stifle efforts made by dreamers to develop to their highest potential and experience success. To be complacent about lack of opportunities for any racial group is against the American ideal, which emphasizes equality for all citizens. According to Hecht, many of the solutions needed to revive America as the land of opportunity, where any one can achieve success are already in place.

Education

To reclaim the American dream, education is critical. Education, once considered the cornerstone of opportunity and upward mobility, needs to be reevaluated. In the 1960s, for example, a free public school and high school diploma were enough to get a good manufacturing job with decent pay to support a family. In the 1970s, only 28 percent of jobs required more than high school education. However, because of advances in technology and economic changes, millions of low-skill jobs have vanished (Carnavale, Smith & Stroll, 2013). It was projected that by the year 2020, 65 percent of jobs will require education beyond high school diploma. Based on current trends, this project seems accurate.

As the labor market continues to grow, it is imperative that everyone has access to quality education to thrive in the twenty-first century and beyond. For example, many states and the federal government are already enabling thousands of Americans to earn college credits and degrees successfully and effectively from the comfort of their homes. It is also recommended that the entire education system be fixed where it is broken so that every citizen, regardless of race, income, or gender, to acquire the skills needed to excel. Education provides the tool to mold our American values which is the key to remain productive and successful.

Many of the aspects of the good life as expressed by the founding fathers rest on a belief in the importance of education. As the founding fathers crafted the Declaration of Independence and the Constitution of the United States, they didn't believe that great societies were created by wealth, but through education (High, 20 15).

Thomas Jefferson agreed with Adams about the influence of education and maintained that the best society was created by educating the common people. Education also plays an important role in self-reliance which is necessary to pursue self – interest, and experience freedom of choice in decision making. As Jefferson explained in his letter "Crusade Against Ignorance," education is patently important to ensure that people don't get manipulated from lack of knowledge.

In addition, education can enable people to think for themselves and avoid following others blindly. Jefferson believed that the more educated people are, the more capable they are of analyzing issues and forming their own opinions. In short, education enables individuals to maintain their unique personality, a necessary character to achieve American dream.

New insight on the dream

Both native-born Americans and immigrants are fixated on achieving the American dream, symbolizing success. However, in recent times, due to changing economic conditions, the dreams appear elusive to many of our citizens. It becomes necessary to reexamine the factors likely to impact the possibility of realizing the American dream.

As William Greider stated, "the good times as we have known them, are not coming back. Americans needs new vision that helps them deal with the new economic realities." For example, the ideals of American dreamlife – liberty and pursuit of happiness – may not be easily experienced in view of the demanding work schedule and little or no time left to relax and enjoy life. Many believe that the realities of American life need to be redefined.

Even though the threats of scarcity and deprivation have been eliminated, many people are yoked with insatiable desire to accumulate material possessions. As John Maynard Keynes wrote long ago, life is about living wisely and agreeably with the assurance that deprivation is no longer the driving force of existence. According to a British economist, the old economic problem of scarcity and survival have been solved especially for the developed nations, as such people should put aside fear, reduce stress, and learn to enjoy life. Once we are free from overaccumulation of material things and stop worrying, then it becomes possible to discover what it means to be human.

The pursuit of happiness may not be fully realized when people are always busy with little time to rest. According to Greider, what Americans lose in the quest for economic success is the small enjoyment of everyday life, such as having daily dinner with everyone present at the table and having good time.

In terms of freedom, many people are denied a great intangible – the loss of dignity to direct their lives, especially in the business environment. This occurs at work, where people lack the right to speak out freely about decisions impacting their daily lives. Several people are subjected to a system of command and control, and they have no choice but remain silent. In this context it becomes questionable how one can pursue the American dream if they don't have the freedom to express their views,

The definition of progress, success, and prosperity may likely surface in a different form in the years ahead. Gradually lots of people are turning to smaller cars that look like toys and smaller houses with little or no yards, which is a deviation from the way American dream was traditionally defined. People can definitely adjust to the new lifestyle provided they are confident the country is moving towards fulfilling transformation with inclusive purpose.

For the American dream to remain relevant, all future jobs should pay a livable wage rate. Both private and public sector employers should ensure that the minimum wage would be enough for any worker with family to afford basic needs to live a comfortable life. As Franklin Roosevelt described it in the Second Bill of Rights, public jobs that pay more than minimum wages, would likely impact the economy positively and permanently. With this approach, the social consequences could be profound. For example, it would be a direct attack on poverty and financial insecurity. Jobs with decent wages not only bring continuous income into the community but would improve lives and create happy citizens able to achieve American dream.

Future initiatives to keep the dream alive

Here we discuss how our children can prepare through education, community outreach, integration within the society, and creation of job opportunities as well as ventures to grow the economy for the future generation.

In addition to giving back to our community, we also need to ensure that our children devote their best efforts to creating and participating in a more unified and progressive nation. The role of education particularly advance education is indispensable to the creation of a bright future with focus on technology, sciences, management, and leadership.

We need to encourage our young people to engage in industries and technological advancements with potential for growth. In addition, they need to explore new inventions to facilitate production – and increase quality of life for all. The essence is to create awareness of intellectual development which is achievable in a country such as the United States with overwhelming opportunity for entrepreneurship for anyone with the zeal and commitment. The goal here is to recognize that everyone in this country can become an inventor, employer, or a success at any level, based on fundamental work ethic incapsulated in vision, dedication, and perseverance.

Chapter Thirteen

Elements of the American Dream

The dream is a journey to achieve individual interest rooted in experiencing freedom, liberty, and pursuit of happiness. Although personal perspectives may vary, there is consensus that the dream is always driven by hope for the future encapsulated in work ethic. Approximately 87 percent of Americans strongly believe that living the dream, understanding the role of hard work, getting involved in building a more productive society, as well as solving social problems constitute novel paradigms of American dreams. In this section, we shall examine relevant concepts which are known to symbolize the attainment of the American dream. From this, the reader can see what the American dream entails and whether it is actually something that one can achieve in their lifetime.

The new American dream goes beyond the acquisition of material possession to looking out for the less privileged both at home and abroad. It has been observed that many foreigners or immigrants in the country have been sending a portion of their earnings to their loved ones in their home country. Some only come to America so that they can improve the situation of their family members at home. A review of the literature indicates what contributes to personal happiness in Americans. In other words, the pursuit of personal happiness which focused on personal gratification has subsided and morphed into sacrificing personal pleasures evidenced by making financial donations to care for the needy.

Many have traveled across the ocean by land and sea to achieve the American dream. Realistically, not everyone who devoted all the resources available has been able to acknowledge the attainment of the dream. To some who have paid the price through painstaking efforts, hard work, resolve, and persistence, the dream is still achievable. Those who focus on what they want and persist in doing hard work are the ones who have seen some success. They have been able to improve their situation and that of their loved ones significantly.

However, there may be some dreamers who have invested their know-how in hard work and dedication to their careers but lack the understanding of essential components of the package for success. Our goal in this section is to elucidate these components one must acquire to be able to comfortably arrive at the gate which leads to the fulfillment of the dream. The components to be addressed in this section include hope, the importance of assets, savings, homeownership, government role in home ownership, and what it takes to succeed.

Hope

Without hope, we become hopeless, and if nothing is done attainment of goals become impossible (Ezidinma, 2022). Those who have no hope are not able to prosper anywhere in the world. It is hope that drives us in pursuing our goals. It is the fire that drives us in working hard to get what we want. Hope touches the very fabric of our human nature to envision a future laden with, freedom, and happiness to live a robust life on our terms under the rule of law. The American dream is driven by hope. With hope, we are energized with the determination to undertake the journey. That is why we come from all over the world to pursue our interests to the highest potential guided with hope.

In pursuit of the American dream, the first step entails the creation of a mental picture of what we want, how we go about it and the action taken to actualize it, with hard work. That was how America came to be. The founders of this great nation conceived hope which gave birth to the idealism of a free society where every man and woman can achieve success to the best of their abilities without unnecessary restriction. The mental picture we create can help us achieve our goals as it gives us a view of where we want to go. We can then plan out how to achieve this in an effective way.

The next step is to exercise hope and it can only be functional in an environment free from redundant rules and policies designed to cripple initiatives. Some people may feel like these hindrances are present in their homeland and not in America, which is said to be a free country.

Many in this country have been able to surmount obstacles and challenges to get to the peak, made possible because the environment is conducive and formulated to make provisions for dreamers to excel. For anyone serious about achieving the American dream, the role of hope is critical, because, without hope which defines patently our desire, our journey is devoured of purpose and meaning and doomed to be futile. Therefore, anyone who comes to America should be hopeful and positive that what they wish to achieve can actually happen. Without this hope, they can lose track of what they want and become disappointed.

Why hope is important to achieve the dream

Winston Churchill said, "All the great things are simple, and many can be expressed in a single word: freedom, justice, honor, duty, mercy, hope." Hope is what gives us the strength not to quit, to fight for another day even when we don't see the end in sight. It is indeed a powerful thing which can inspire us to pursue the impossible. It is something that helps us carry on when there are tough times.

Hope is the best motivator that keeps the dream alive and fills our hearts with optimism. As Martin Luther King, Jr. said "We must accept finite disappointment, but never lose infinite hope."

Hope is something that limits the feelings of helplessness, limits stress, allows us to increase our happiness, and also improve the quality of life that we are living. Those without hope will be frightened, worried and anxious. There is research which shows that hope can aid us in handling stress and anxiety and helps us cope with adversity. It is something that contributes to our well-being. Hopeful individuals believe that they can influence their goals and achieve the American dream.

Humans will always need clean water, clean air, food to eat, and hope to sustain them. Hope gives life and exhorts us to try different approaches to solve a problem.

Any soul without hope is not living but surviving. In time of difficulty, hope gives us the reason to keep the faith, and move forward.

Hope is the force that can give someone in the gutter a billion-dollar smile on their face, and peace in their hearts, while someone living in a castle feels broken and empty. Hope is pertinent because it is the lifeblood of all things that get done in the world. The decisions we make every day are fueled with hope in our hearts to experience better outcomes. New relationships are triggered because we hope for loving experiences filled with peace, joy, and happiness.

The Civil Rights Movement in America was imbued with hope – the hope that all humans should be treated with equality. Hope drove all the protests and ushered in victory. This movement was mainly involved with empowering Black Americans by introducing legislation that would end segregation, Black voter suppression as well as discriminatory employment.

Walk with hope in your heart and you will never walk alone. Just because you had a bad day or you had an unpleasant encounter with someone, don't lose your hope in humanity – I assure you this, people are good-natured. With hope, sooner or later someone will make you smile again.

Hope gives us a reason to dream and brings out the best in us. We wake up to pursue daily activities, organized and presented to us by hope, and when we do our best, the outcome often turns into inner fulfillment manifested in joy, peace, and happiness (Azhar, 2021)

Our collective hope for America is our invisible link fortified with a united spirit, to sustain a country ever evolving with innovative ideas for the betterment of all of us.

Importance of assets

In the pursuit of the American dream, the role of asset accumulation is of vital importance. Assets can be said to be something of value, like property and equipment. Assets development through savings often represents long-term economic security, which forms the bases for wealth (Shobe & Narine, 2005). Asset development through savings and investment lay the foundation to become financially independent which could lead to wealth. The wealth, in terms of financial independence, is an important measure of overall economic well-being, which directly influences the ability of immigrants to successfully integrate into the host country's society. Realistically, wealth is often used to create opportunities, and secure a standard of living and could be passed from generation to generation (Shobe & Narine, 2005). From these quotes one can deduce that assets are important and need to be handled carefully if one is to live a peaceful life.

The prevailing paradigm suggests that income and assets are different forms of the same source. However, while income meets current consumption needs, assets meet future financial needs. Income alone is not an adequate measure of well-being unless some of it is invested to meet long-term needs. It is important to create awareness of the strategies that could gradually enable immigrants to generate wealth. Immigrants need to know the importance of saving their income and converting it into valuable assets that they can use and also help their families.

Importance of savings

America was founded by successive waves of different immigrants, each of these contributed their ambition along with talents to make a better life for their families and the nation as a whole. The drive to get a better life in this new land usually makes immigrants want to work hard. It is a type of dedication to increase one's financial resources.

Financial and investment consultants maintain that continuous savings over a long time is a simple strategy anyone could adopt to create wealth and achieve their dreams. Research studies indicate that one of the most important ways to accumulate assets in the United States is through savings. Abundant information exists regarding how middle and upper-income native-born individuals save money. Saving money is important. It allows one to have financial security and even freedom. It secures them when there is a financial emergency. However, how low-income foreign-born immigrants save has not been fully understood.

In the 2017 Kauffman Entrepreneurship Index, it was seen that immigrants tend to be more entrepreneurial in comparison to native-born Americans. On top of this it has been seen that immigrants employ credit less often when buying stuff like cars, homes, etc. This is why they have lower levels of debt when compared to native-born Americans.

According to Dorantes and Poxo (2002), most immigrants tend to have low wealth than native-born Americans. This finding can be partially explained because most immigrants tend to send money back home to their native countries, even when they earn low wages here in the United States. Immigrants also tend to have more precautionary savings with the intent to offset future economic difficulties. This behavior may be associated with the higher risk involved with living in a foreign land, as well as labor market instability, and financial and health-related crisis. Accessibility to financial structures is known to motivate both native and foreign-born immigrants to engage in aggressive saving, which is essential to achieving the American dream. For example, Community Development Union is one of the financial institutions known to assist most immigrants to develop the habit of savings. CDUs are self-sustaining financial institutions that actively serve economically vulnerable – racially and ethnically diverse communities.

Home ownership

Owing a home is one of the accomplishments in terms of achieving the American dream. In addition, for most people in the United States, home ownership is the most important asset for the family or an individual. In 1993, home equity accounted for 44 percent of the house value in the United States, and 64 percent owned their homes. Some of the benefits of homeownership include improved accommodation, tax benefits, and pride in home. Homeowners tend to hold more wealth than renters (Shobe & Narine, 2005). For example, in 1999, the asset poverty rate among homeowners was approximately 6 percent, while the poverty rate for renters was 67 percent.

There is no law present which says that non-U.S. residents are not able to own property in America. A research found out that Miami was the city which has the highest level of immigrant homeownership and also the largest percentage of immigrants within its population. It was seen that the highest immigrant homeownership rates were actually in some of the costliest markets. This is not surprising as these areas have vibrant economies and also job opportunities therefore attracting immigrants.

Other benefits of home ownership include the accumulation of equity and saving from renting a house or apartment.

Unlike renters, who often reside in neighborhoods for a short period, homeowners tend to contribute to the neighborship in which they live by participating in activities designed to increase the quality and property value in the neighborhood (Camarota, 2011). Home ownership is positively associated with physical health, with homeowners reporting lower rates of smoking, lung cancer, and admission to nursing homes.

It is recommended that immigrants should understand the importance of owning a home as a way to build wealth and prepare for future economic security. Studies indicate that most immigrants have a limited understanding of the benefits of homeownership. For example, immigrant homeownership rates have decreased from 1970 to 2000, with only 46 percent owning their homes. On the other hand, native-born homeownership rates have increased steadily with approximately 70 percent owning their homes in 2000, compared to 63 percent in 1970 (Camorata, 2001). Interestingly, data show that immigrants with medium income have homes higher in value than native-born. For example, the mean value for native-born homes was $107,000 while that of foreign-born was $163,000.

The government's role in home ownership

There is a popular misconception present that foreigners as well as non-citizens are not able to buy a home in America. However, this is not true. While a person's residency status can determine if they will get certain loans, there are many home-buying options available.

The government has a critical role to play to enable its citizen to achieve the American dream, by creating an environment conducive to individuals developing to their potential. Some skeptics question whether the government, particularly the federal government, is aiding or hindering its citizens in realizing their dream. The fact is that the federal government has programs in place to assist Americans with home ownership.

Every year, June is dedicated as National Home Ownership month. House and Urban Development (HUD), endeavors to support and expand homeownership opportunities for all Americans year-round. Ideally, owning a home is regarded as an attainment of the facet of the American dream. Owning a home conveys several economic benefits such as the ability to accumulate wealth and build up credit through home equity.

According to the U.S. Census Bureau, home ownership fell from 66.2 percent in 2000 to 64.4 percent in 2017. Many Americans are not confident that they will ever own a home. Studies indicate that many first-time home buyers have difficulty coming up with the down payment. These challenges are even more pronounced for minorities whose ownership rate of 43.3 percent remains substantially below that of whites.

Assistance Program – HUD has initiated housing counseling for first-time home buyers as one possible solution. Another initiative is the Family Self Sufficiency (FFS) program, which helps low-income families to receive rent subsidies. Participants work with a case manager over five years to set goals related to education, job training, money management, childcare, and transportation.

Homeownership has been promoted as government policy not only through FHA loans, but also through government-sponsored entities such as Freddie Mac, Fannie Mae, and Federal Home Bank. In addition, the federal government promotes home ownership through the tax deduction for mortgage interest payments on a primary residence. To enable citizens to own their homes, it is the policy of the government to increase homeownership rates and the economic benefits that home ownership conveys. Permanent residents and also green card holders do have access to similar mortgage financing choices like U.S. citizens.

Green card holders may be able to get a home with only 3% down payment. They are able to get the same loan services as U.S. citizens, such as FHA loans along with other government-backed services like Freddie Mac.

This book delves into issues of home ownership to create awareness about the opportunities the government and its agencies have in place for legal immigrants and citizens to own their homes, in their quest to achieve part of the American dream. HUD promised to assist potential home buyers who qualify and meet the requirements, with the opportunity to become homeowners.

What it takes for immigrants to succeed

The impression in other countries is that the United States is a land filled with milk and honey, where success is readily attainable. We focus on the beauty of the American dream, by evaluating what it takes to achieve it and maintain it (Propal, 2022. But contrary to expectations, several immigrants become aware of the reality of the efforts needed to achieve the American dream after arriving in the new land. The truth starts to emerge regarding the enormous sacrifice required to survive and succeed. And the fact is that many immigrants have achieved the American dream but still struggle to make ends meet.

Recent immigrants as well as their kids are a growing part of the country. Immigrants pursue various paths so as to become economically successful. This includes stuff like starting a business or working in various occupations. The better-educated immigrants are the ones who have greater incomes.

A review of the literature provides relevant insights into how immigrants, as well as native-born Americans, could ameliorate the opportunity in their environment to better their lives. The question becomes: What challenges do immigrants face when they get to the United States in other to assimilate into the society and find success? For many, the first challenge is a communication problem. According to Pew research, as of 2018, almost half of the immigrants in the country are not English proficient. Learning a new language takes time. It takes a long time for adults to learn and speak any new language fluently. It is easier for children and young adults to learn and fluently speak a new language than older adults (Propel. 2121).

With communication problems, many immigrants who are professionals are not able to find employment in their fields, even with advanced degrees. Such situations decrease the chances of appropriate employment opportunities which results in acceptance of low wages and loss of extra income. For example, there are cases of African immigrants who are doctors, lawyers, engineers, and highly educated individuals who end up taking low-skilled jobs to generate income for their families or face further hardship. This type of situation is prevalent and some of those affected try to improve their English which in some cases is not good enough to gain employment at the executive level.

It has been observed that the children of immigrants who are proficient in English and are generally successful when in school. They are able to do better in schools if their U.S. education can build on their ethnic heritage and when they stay away from detrimental areas of American culture. However, those students who were not able to finish high school are more likely to go to jail.

Financially, poor communication could impact the ability to generate enough income to meet up with daily expenses and save for retirement, plus putting aside money for the children's education. These obstacles could be overcome by immigrants with intense motivation to re-establish their lives and create a brighter future for their children. The caveat here is that success is not guaranteed; on the other hand, not every immigrant is stuck in low-paying jobs forever.

Foreign-born immigrants face challenges in education in terms of receiving assistance and support from family, unlike native-born Americans. The difference is that native-born Americans have all types of educational resources readily. For example, native-born Americans receive support financially and emotionally from parents from preschool age through high school and college. Other advantages include help with schoolwork at home, understanding the American educational school system, and managing key milestones like taking the SAT, or college application, not worrying about school loans because parents have taken care of them (Propal, 2022).

Despite huge differences with the first generation, a major intergenerational progress has been seen in educational attainment. The second-generation members of many contemporary immigrants' groups actually meet and exceed the schooling level of certain third generation native-born Americans.

In addition, network opportunities that are critical to establishing profitable connections are limited to most immigrants. For example, social connections that lead to job opportunities, internships with major corporations, gaining entry into high institutions, with the ability to stay in expensive cities and not worry about paying huge bills, because the family is there to provide support, could become helpful.

Immigrant men do attain higher employment rates compared to their second-generation counterparts. The employment advantage can be mostly seen in the least-educated immigrants. They are more likely to attain employment than educated native-born men. The groups that have low-status occupations within the first generation have been seen to improve their educational status much in the second generation, but they still are not equal with the third-generation Americans. This is why it can be seen that immigrants are able to improve their situation in the country.

Native-born Americans are more likely to receive training in financial management and investing which is essential to building wealth and achieving the American dream (Propal, 2022). Lack of basic understanding of financial strategies to build up investment portfolios by several immigrants is blamed for poor retirement savings, with little reserve to meet up escalating daily expenses. An equitable educational system and government policies could equip immigrants to understand and take advantage of programs designed to provide information on The National Bureau of Economic Research did a study which was published in 2019. It looked at different father-son pairs of immigrants. It was s observed that children of immigrants tended to have higher rates of upward mobility in comparison to children of those who were born within the U.S. They found that shifts within immigration policy and even country of origin did not change the pattern. This is true even if the first generation was poor or relatively well-off.

financial issues (Propal, 2022)

It is more complicated to see what occurs after the second generation, but the initial immigrant upward mobility is still apparent. Those who have seen upward mobility happen in their family often think that the promises have been kept of the American dream. Hard work along with education yielded better outcomes for their kids, with more stability occurring for the family. There are many stories about migrants who have been a very successful in America.

Drawing from experience, immigrants have also a personal responsibility to educate themselves on financial management for their future. The dream is attainable to those who understand the commitment and hard work involved to make it to the finish line. For example, serious efforts must be exacted to build generational wealth, climb the social-economic ladder, develop social connections, and participate in community development projects. Along this continuum, immigrants have ample opportunity to thrive in America.

Chapter Fourteen

Giving back to the United States

Giving back to the community or the country benefits the giver and the recipient. It solidifies our commonalities and ushers in a sense of unity and leaves us in peace and harmony. The pursuit of the American dream has led to giving back to the society or community by many who have been successful in their careers. Many philanthropic organizations believe that giving back to the community is the most important and valuable action anyone can take.

Giving back entails providing resources for free to those who are in need, without expecting anything in return. Giving back should not have any benefits to the giver, no recognitions or accolades. The sole reward is that the giver feels he or she has made a significant contribution to someone's life. It is important to emphasize that anyone can give back to the community. Giving is not solely the prerogative of a privileged class or socio-economic status. It is an act of appreciation and a way to show that other people's well-being is equally important.

Immigrants enter America with the dream to getting a better life for themselves along with their families. They do not represent a threat to the democracy of the country; they reinforce the values which make up America. America is a country made and built with the help of immigrants. Throughout its history, immigrants who are looking for a better life have come into the country. They have been able to reinvigorate the labor force, enrich America's cultural fabric, as well as make democracy stronger in the country.

The United States is the most philanthropic country in the world, and the benefits are enormous. Some people may want to give back but are not sure how to get started. You can start today. The first step is to think about what cause you like to support. For example, if you are interested in children, find the area of philanthropy that speaks to your heart. There are schools in the community that may need volunteers to raise money for various needs as well as children's hospitals that may need financial donations for new equipment and research studies. As you give back, not only that your good deeds benefit those on the receiving end, but knowing that you are making a difference in other people's lives is the most pertinent reward for achieving the American dream.

Whilst all successive waves of immigration increase the unique blend of culture which defines the country, it is wrong to think that immigrants are a threat to American values. Today's immigrants, similar to our forefathers, arrive in the country looking for the ability to worship freely and express themselves without the threat of government retribution. They want to chart their own economic future. The immigrants who have seen oppression and lack of freedom do not undermine America's value but embrace it. The diversity of the country contributes to its economic vitality. The companies that they established create jobs, promote innovation, and help the country's economic productivity.

Rather than weakening America's values and democracy like some people think, immigrants enrich and even revitalize the country's institutions and beliefs. Whilst people come as Mexicans, Russians, Chinese, etc., as time passes, they become Americans.

Patriotism

The United States of America deserves my patriotic support, and I will render my unwavering dedication to be of service in any capacity to my country. Any citizen who is true to being an American must be patriotic to the United States because it is a reflection of giving back to the country. President John F. Kennedy once said, "Ask for what you can do for your country and not what your country can do for you." This statement resonated with people not only in the United States but all over the world. Given all the opportunities, and constitutional acts designed to allow citizens their rights to pursue individual dreams, it makes sense to defend and protect our union.

Patriotism is a concept that brings people together to express their dedication and love for their country. It is a shared sense of solidarity and love for our country. Patriotism allows for the collective expression of commitment to achieve the common goal on behalf of our country. Patriotism can be said to be a feeling of love, devotion, and a sense of belonging to one's country.

The basic tenet of patriotism is to do what is right to show support for the country. The act of patriotism is a signal to other countries to express how much we value and love our country, and how united we are to support our country.

The act of patriotism and the feeling that comes with it portray the extent to which citizens appreciate and are motivated to come to the defense of their country. There are various ways to show patriotism for the country such as displaying the flag, wearing hats, and shirts made with the flag, supporting the military, volunteering to help military families, and joining paramilitary units or joining the military to defend the country. According to excerpts from Lake Oconee, Boomers here are other ways to show patriotism to our country.

- **Be an Active Citizen and Focus on Current Events:** To show love for your country and stay current with what is going on in your region and other parts of the world. Remain informed about what is going on in political issues and how it can impact you. Your opinion is valuable for policymakers to formulate effective strategies for national security.

- **Vote:** If one wants to honor the principles on which the country was built, they should vote. Volunteering to work the polls when an election is going on is helpful.

- **Participate:** Endeavor to participate in your local legislative committee, attend meetings and talk about relevant issues in need of a solution.

- **Visit Historic Museums:** Find a local museum that displays various parts of American history to learn something new about the early stages of the history of this country. Get informed about the challenges and obstacles our founding fathers endured to lay the foundation for this great nation.

- **Venerate the Veterans:** Many Americans fought and died for our country. Others fought for their country and are still alive, some are wounded and remaining in the hospital. Pay respect to them and salute veterans. Consider taking time during the day to visit memorials to show respect for their sacrifices. If you know of anyone who was a veteran of wars like the Korean and Vietnam wars, you can take out time to help them out. It is simple activities that can help like mowing their lawns, taking them to a pharmacy, shopping, etc. Thank veterans for their commitments to stand up for their support and to give their lives to defend the country.

- **Serve on a Jury:** To serve in a jury is to show patriotism, which indicates support and willingness to ensure that you are in support of law and order. Agreeing to a juror implies acceptance of responsibility to contribute to the effort to ensure that citizens are treated fairly under the law without bias.
- **Support the National Parks:** Consider paying a visit to your national park to donate to support them. Some parks are short of help because of budget cuts, and they are not able to provide services to visitors, due to a lack of funds to pay more workers.
- **Fly the flag properly:** It is important to fly the Stars and Stripes right. People need to know that the S. Flag Code comes with strict guidelines concerning how to display as well as handle the flag. Find out what these are and follow them.

Benefits of Being Patriotic

Patriotism is about having strong love and dedication to appreciate one's country and the willingness to sacrifice one's life for the country. Individuals may have their own definitions, but in general it is about putting the interest of the country before individual interest. There are numerous benefits individuals could experience by being patriotic to their country. According to Robbins (2018), here are some of the benefits that individuals could realize.

Patriotism is something which we can understand even whether we experience it in a different way. There are different ways that Americans participate in showing patriotism as said above. Whilst the people of America engage in different acts of patriotism, it is necessary to understand how this can contribute to our national identity.

Self-motivation

To be patriotic towards one's country is beneficial, as it motivates the individual to undertake their day-to-day activities as a show of support to their countries in terms of contributing to productivity. This type of attitude in turn creates a feeling of self-fulfillment, for getting involved in the welfare of the country. For those who find being patriotic to their country as an obligation, being engaged in any form of economic activity is critically important, as it provides the participant with inner confidence of assisting to create an environment with potential opportunities. The self-motivation that comes with being patriotic is important because it reminds individuals of their responsibility to be model citizens and to uphold the law at all times and at all costs.

Productivity

Being patriotic could drive an individual to contribute passionately towards supporting their country in any way possible to solve problems. In most cases, individuals who work hard to promote patriotism reap the benefits by maintaining an optimistic outlook for the future of the country. In that regard, when the country flourishes economically, the individuals enjoy the benefits. Some of our leaders have utilized the concept of economic productivity to appeal to patriotism.

President Kennedy in his famous speech connected the relationship between productivity and patriotism by saying "Ask not what your country can do for you, but ask what you can do for your country." This appeal was meant to promote the productivity of patriotic citizens (Robbins, 2018).

Promote Better Governance

Leadership encapsulated in patriotic ideals is likely to energize the people and promote good governance. Patriotic people often work hard to ensure that the country is well governed. They speak out when leaders abuse their office in situations such as racism, police brutality, bribery, corruption, scandals, or bad governance. For instance, it was for the sake of patriotism that Martin Luther King Jr. fought for years to promote equality for all races in the United States.

Enhance Social Cohesion and Peace

In a country where the majority of the citizens uphold patriotism, in most cases, everybody encourages each other to achieve a common goal by participating in activities that improve society, ensure better living standards, and promote peace and racial harmony. Patriotic individuals tend to promote the rule of law and seek to find a solution when it comes to conflict resolution, thereby preventing anyone from taking the law into their hands.

Patriotism is therefore a concept that brings individuals together. The sense of solidarity as well as love for the country tends to be a sentiment that binds. This is a shared feeling along with common goal to pursue what is best for the country.

Togetherness is something which helps the country. This may be something like coming together during the COVID-19 pandemic or supporting one another when there is a natural disaster. Patriotism is what inspires us to help one another when they need it.

Selfless Service to others and the Country

Patriotic individuals derive joy by devoting their lives to the service of their country and such individuals are equally recognized as national heroes and venerated with high esteem. In the military, some soldiers have been decorated with "purple hearts" because they risked their lives to rescue fellow soldiers who have been wounded by the enemy. Most people who joined the military during World War I and 2 including the Vietnam War did so on the bases of patriotism because they love their country.

Stronger nation

Patriotism is what makes a nation stronger. You can relate better to others in the country that you share and when there are more people who are patriotic, the stronger the country will be. Those people who are patriotic aim to do what is right for the country in supporting it to become stronger. When there are patriotic sentiments, we know that anything can be overcome.

The American dreamers are grateful: They give back

The ideological frameworks which are rooted in liberty, individual freedom of choice, and pursuit of happiness, were the catalysts people needed to develop to their highest potential.

American dream provides hope for dreamers all over the world to come and participate to build a nation where one could achieve success based on their unique ability. The desire to live in a free country with equality and opportunity convinced millions of immigrants from all over the world to leave their native country for the new land. Every year many immigrants come to America, speaking a different language and facing new hurdles. Some challenges can be access to health care, education, employment, and more.

Because many Americans have succeeded in achieving the American dream, much societal good has been realized through the practice of giving back to communities and the country. Americans are the most generous givers to their fellow citizens to help them in times of need. The American dream endures because it challenges and expects the best from every dreamer.

Many pursue the American dream not only for personal success but to extend their blessings to those around them, here in the United States and across the globe. In addition, those who have been fortunate are willing to reach out, to create opportunities for others. Various economic and social programs are made possible by successful dreamers. Such programs need to be elucidated to illustrate the importance of breeding dreamers in our country.

Immigrants help the economy of America in different ways. They work at high rates as well as make up much of the workforce in certain industries. The geographic mobility they have aids local economies in handling worker shortages. In this way they smooth out hurdles present in the economy which can harm it. Immigrant workers are able to support aging native-born Americans by increasing the number of workers in comparison to retirees. In this way they can enhance the Social Security and Medicare trust funds.

Giving back to the community could come from businesses and individuals. In most cases, businesses give money to different causes to help the needy meet their financial issues. Sometimes money is donated to help families with loved ones in the hospital to pay medical bills. Other ways businesses give back to the community include raising money from their customers as well as adding their donations to the money collected to make a significant contribution to major causes such as victims of fire, floods, and hurricanes.

Volunteering is another way to give back to the community. Although volunteering or offering your service might seem like hard work, countless rewards come with it. By connecting to others through volunteering, the community is enriched with caring and responsible individuals. Serving others is an opportunity to take your mind away from personal issues, and to connect with others to gain new experiences and an enhanced worldview.

To volunteer time to help others is rewarding and never to be regretted. When it comes to giving back, what matters is the desire to participate in doing good regardless of the amount donated or hours spent helping someone. Many businesses and individuals that I know personally including my family give back to the community to affirm their gratitude for the opportunity to achieve the American dream.

The importance of giving back to the community

Giving back to the community or the country benefits the giver and the recipient. It solidifies our commonalities and ushers in a sense of unity, helping us to live in peace and harmony. The pursuit of the American dream has led to giving back to the society or community by many who have been successful in careers. Many philanthropic organizations believe that giving back to the community is the most important and valuable action anyone can take.

Giving back to the community and country is an important way for parents to teach their children the importance of caring and sharing. Whilst growing up as a teenager, my parents got me involved in delivering various gifts to the needy in the city. It was a sobering experience. It was interesting to observe the smile on recipients' faces.

Giving back entails providing resources for free to those who are in need, without expecting anything in return. Giving back should not have any benefits to the giver, nor recognition or accolades. The sole reward is that the giver feels he or she has made a significant contribution to someone's life. It is important to emphasize that anyone can give back to the community. Giving is not only the prerogative of a privileged class or socio-economic status. It is an act of appreciation and a way to show that other people's well-being is equally important.

Giving back can enrich your life, help you in familiarizing with your particular community, and connect you to individuals and ideas which can positively impact your perspective. Helping your community gives you the chance to grow as an individual and to better comprehend how you fit in the world.

(This section needs to be deleted because it is repeated)

The dream lives on for good.

The American dream is a cultural legacy crafted with the inert human aspiration to excel and be the best one can be, not just for personal gratification but to build a prosperous society, where individuals are not afraid to reach their highest potential. Thomas Adam in his book *The Epic of the Nation* captured a reflective image of the new America with the following statement. He described a nation where there is equality, attainment of happiness is encouraged, and hard work is rewarded with success.

For the American dream to endure and remain relevant to future generations, it must be nurtured and guided to represent meaningful endeavors, to perpetuate a loving and peaceful society where fairness and justice are unquestionable. To keep the dream on the clear path, it must not be contaminated with greed, fixation on material possession, or isolation, but rather encapsulated in unity and harmony. One of the most common means many successful dreamers utilize to show their gratitude to society is giving back to the community.

America is one of the few countries which can give people the result of their hard work. In fact, Abraham Lincoln was born inside a log cabin and did not get a formal judicial education. However, he was still able to become a popular lawyer and Commander in Chief. Oprah Winfrey grew up in poverty and now is one of the richest people in the world. The beauty of the country is in the determination of the people to fulfill the American dream. The country is a land full of opportunities. This is why hard work and determination pays off here.

Lessons Learned from achieving the American dream

Every morning when I wake up and get through with my devotion, I turn to look at the American flag as a reminder that we are blessed to live in a nation where the opportunities exist to actualize our biggest dreams. I came to the United States with the determination to acquire education, knowing that it is the gateway to creating a brighter future. Even with financial difficulties and other challenges, I promised to my family back home that I would not drop out of college. This promise kept me grounded. After graduation, I applied the same approach of setting goals and achieving them to tackle both business and personal issues. Here are pertinent lessons gleaned from the experience in the quest to achieve the American dream. Utilizing these lessons has helped navigate challenges and impediments to moving forward, and hopefully, you will find them informative. I learned these lessons whilst staying in America and trying to fulfill the American dream like many other immigrants.

Never quit.

No matter how tough it is, it is important to remain steadfast and not quit. This is something that those pursuing the American dream need to keep in mind. There are many times when one may feel like quitting due to tough situations that they face. However, if they give in to this temptation, they will not be able to be successful. I faced different challenges but always tried to continue moving on no matter how difficult it was for me.

One of my employees, a Vietnam veteran named Charles, gave me a gift: a plaque with a heading that read "Don't quit." What impressed me about Charles is the fact that he was always ready to tackle any task with a positive attitude. Even though he was wounded in the Vietnam War – shot in the leg and unable to walk straight – he would not want to be classified as disabled. Both of us had the same attitude of staying the course, no matter how painful the experience, until the task is completed. During the recession of 2002, many businesses folded up and several people were unemployed, and it was tough to make ends meet. The business was slow, but we managed to utilize the resources at our disposal to survive.

We were in the construction industry and because of the recession, people were laid off. Many homeowners lost their jobs and could not pay their mortgages. Foreclosures were ubiquitous and house prices were as low as they could get. New construction projects were on hold. Residential as well as commercial projects came to a stand-still. It was a tough period to stay in business, but we were resilient and refused to close the business. When the tough times became unbearable, I read my bible and read some words on the plaque Charles gave to me.

Here are my favorite passages from the plaque written by an anonymous author.

"When things go wrong as they will sometimes. When the road you're trudging seems uphill. When the funds are low, and the debts are high, and you want to smile, but sigh. When care is pressing you down a bit, rest if you must, but don't you quit.

Life is queer with its twists and turns. As everyone of us sometimes learns. Many a failure turns about. When he might have won had he stuck it out. Don't give up though the pace seems slow. You may succeed with another blow.

Success is failure turned inside out. The silver tint of the clouds of doubt. And you never can tell how close you are. It may be near when it seems so far. So, stick to the fight when you are hardest hit. It is when things seem worse that you must not quit."

With these encouraging words, it was possible to maintain sanity and composure to sustain the business until eventually the economy turned around and our business picked up. We survived and we received a generous financial reward.

During my academic years, there were times when the pressure and stress from assignments and workload accumulated to a breaking point. Completing the doctorate program was particularly challenging given research projects and running a business that required intense attention. On some occasions, I had decided to put it on hold and focus on the business, but prudent advice from family and my chair energized me to delve into the research projects and get them completed. There are many people facing this same situation and those who have quit were not able to remain in the country. It is important to remain focused on your main goal and ignore any issues that come in the way of achieving it.

I owe much gratitude to loved ones who provided moral support which was necessary to overcome difficult times. To anyone who may be facing tough times, challenges and tribulations, this testimony is to exhort you to be strong, determined and assured that whatever mountain that is on your way will eventually dissolve into oblivion. With resolve and dedication, you will achieve the American dream. Just remember, no matter the stress level: DON'T QUIT.

For me, these words have been influential, and I hope they can help others out as well. Whatever one does and whatever situation they are faced with, they need to remember one thing: Don't quit. There are many examples of immigrants who faced really tough times but kept going. These stories can encourage others to also continue moving forward.

Enjoy what you do and seek to do your best.

Pursue your interest. If you don't just make a decent living, but also derive joy and fulfillment, you are more likely to establish happy customers with a positive and loyal attitude towards your organization. Business growth in most cases is a result of word-of-mouth advertising. Satisfied customers tell their families, co-coworkers, and friends about your company and encourage them to utilize your product or services. The enthusiasm and attention directed towards providing quality services to the customer could be rewarding. Customers often notice and appreciate quality services when they are rendered and are likely to become repeat customers. In anything that you do, you should be mindful of what you enjoy, so that you can do your best and succeed.

How you communicate and handle customer relations is important for business success. When customers perceive that the business owner and the staff enjoy providing quality services to please them, it sends the signal that the customer is valued as a person and a contributor to the organization's survival and financial well-being. The decision to engage in a business or career that one is passionate about is a key factor to achieving the American dream.

Whatever you are doing, it is important to enjoy it, or else you will not be motivated to continue moving forward. When you decide to start a business in this country, you will see that there is much competition present in all industries. You need to be able to stand out here. This can be done by giving a good impression to customers that you are confident and can provide them with the services that they are looking for. If you do this, you can stay on the path towards achieving the American dream.

Leveraging our commonalities

After years in the business world as an entrepreneur, I realized that as American citizens we are committed to the preservation of our democracy – our freedom to pursue our dreams and develop to our highest potential. In addition, we have a unique understanding of working together to achieve goals far greater than if we are isolated. This type of attitude is a necessary tenet to become productive and be a part of progress. Without this attitude, one can be distracted from the course that they are pursing.

The lessons I gleaned by understanding the make-up of the society were rewarding in terms of having a successful enterprise and enjoying human relations, which were enriching and emotionally fulfilling. The point here is that by putting into consideration peoples' backgrounds, such as ethnicity and culture, it becomes easier to relate and bond with them. Due to the nature of my business, the opportunity to interact with people from every ethnicity was prevalent, as was the opportunity to put into practice behaviors and communication skills known to elicit positive outcomes. It worked in every scenario. When people are treated with respect and understanding, and as humans, the result is always a better relationship.

I was apprehensive about dealing with individuals from other ethnic groups in my early years in business. Negative stories about interracial conflicts in the news media had an impact on how I perceived relations with those outside my racial group. However, I refused to generalize people's behavior based on their race, because I have experienced acceptance and friendly overture even from strangers who are from different racial groups. With time and after years of analyses of human behavior, it became apparent that how we perceive others is dependent on a preconceived notion. These preconceived notions can affect the way that we deal with others in the community. Once I became convinced that people have fundamentally similar needs and want to live in peace and harmony with their neighbors, it made living in America more enjoyable. It also made it easier to develop relationships. By living in an environment characterized by amicable attitude and cooperative gestures, it becomes possible for individuals to reach their highest potential which is the channel to achieve the American dream.

Living and operating in a diversified community became a source of acquiring cultural education and understanding a second or third language. Through community events during which people from different ethnic groups shared their culinary skills, it became clear that every ethnic dish was unique and special, which contributed to our national heritage. As people gathered during the summer for festivals, it offered an opportunity to appreciate the beauty of individual talents displayed through arts and crafts.

Those who want to achieve the American dream need to keep in mind that the country is full of many people from different cultures and backgrounds. It is necessary to accept everyone if you are to succeed in what you want to do. It takes some time to get comfortable dealing with strangers, but the icebreaker is recognizing that everyone is uniquely dispositioned, and if approached correctly, everybody has something to offer the world. This can be achieved through treating people with respect, and acceptance.

References

Acock, A.C. & Demo, D.H. (1994). Family Diversity and, well - being. Thousand Oak, CA. Sage

Amato, P.R. & Booth, A. (1997). A Generation at Risk: Growing up at an Era of Upheaval. Cambridge, MA Harvard University Press

Anderson, D.R. & Houston, A. (2001). Early childhood television viewing and adolescent behavior. Monograph of the society for research in child development. 264, vol. (66)

Beckett, T. (2016). What could actually work to fix gun violence in America and what doesn't. Retrieved from https://www.theguardian.com/us-news/2016/jun/23/gun-control-violence-what-works-what-doesnt

Benner, C. & Pastor, R. (2015). Brother can you spare a dime. Prosperity and social inclusion in America. Metro Repos. Urban Studies 52(7), 1339-56.

Biblariz, E. & Gottainer, G. (2000). Family Structure and Children's Success: A Comparison of Widowed and Divorced Single Mothers. Journal of Marriage and Family, 62(2)

Carnevalle, P.A., Smith, N. & Stroll, J. (2013). Recovery: Job Growth and Education Requirement through 2020. Georgetown Public Policy Institute Center on Education and the Workforce. June 2013 (https://cewgeorgetown.edu/wapcount/upload/2014/11/Recovery 2020. ES_web-pdf)

Caumont, A. & Cohn, D. (2016). 10 demographic Trends that are shaping the United States and the world. (www.pewresearch.org-fast-tank/2016/03/31/10-10demographic-trends-trends-that-are-shaping-the world)

Cherlin, A.J. (1995). Parental Divorce and Demographic Outcome in Young Adulthood. Demography 32-299-318

Christian, T. & Moffit, L. (2006). Workplace diversity and Group relations. An overview. Group process and Intergroup Relations, 9(4) 459-456

Clark, A.V. (2003). Immigrants and the American dream Excerpts from Guilford Publication.

CMS (2017). Venezuela in crisis. The flight of Venezuela refugees. Retrieved from

Cook, P.J. (1997). Gun in America. Private survey of gun ownership and use of guns. National Institute of Justice

Cuipans, R. (2012). Peer-led and adult-led drug prevention. A meta-analytical comparison. Journal of Drug 2002 (3292), 103-119

D'Amico, P. (2016). Attitude determines our success or failure. Retrieved from https://www.thegibsonsedge.com/blog/attitude-determines-our-success-or-failure

Daley, M. & Wilson, M. (1985). Child Abuse and Other Risks of not Living with Both Parents. Ethology Sociobiology 6, 197-210

DeSilver, D. (2019). Immigrants don't make up majority of workers. Retrieved from https://pewresearch.org/2017/03/17/-from-low-mark-up-majority-of-work

Dike, P. (2013). The impact of workplace diversity in an organization. Department of International Business. Retrieved from: https://core.ac.uk.pdf

Emma, L. (2018). Advantages and disadvantages of diversity in the workplace. Retrieved from:

Esty, K.C. & Hirsh, R. (1995) Workplace Diversity. Retrieved from

Felita, E. & Renwick, B. (2020). The U.S. Immigration Debate Retrieved from htps://cfr.org/background/immigration-debate-/o

Fisher, H. (1992). Anatomy of Love. A Natural History of Matting, Marriage and, why we Stray. George P. Murdock 1949.Socail structure (New York-McMillian).-american -dream/

Fleweling, R. & Bewman, I. (1990). Marriage Structure as a Predictor of Initial Substance Abuse. Journal of Marriage and the Family, 520: 171-181

Fowler, J.S. & Volkow, D.N. (2007). Imagining the addicted human brain. Sci Pract 3(2)4-16. Doi:10.1151/spp07324

Greider, W. (2009). The future of the American. Retrieved from https://www.thenation.com/article/archive/future-american-dream/

Gross, T. (2017). A forgotten History of how the US Government Segregated America https://npr.org/2017/05/03/526655831/a-forgotten-history-of-how-the u-s-government-segregated -america

Griswold, D. (2002). Immigrants have enriched American culture and enhanced our influence in the world. Retrieved from: cata.org/publication/commentary/immigrats-have-enriched-american-culture

Haynie, D. (2014). The number of international students continues to climb. Retrieved from http://www.usnews.com

Headd, B. (2010) Analysis of small business and jobs. U.S. Small Business Administration. Brown Office of Advocacy

Heath, S. (1996). Marital Joy Linked to Good Health. Retrieved from: https://www.researchgate.net. The Age, Nov.30

Hecht, B.L. (1959). Reclaiming American dream: proven solution for creating economic opportunity for all. Retrieved from: https://www.amazon.com.

Hepburn, L. (2004). Firearm availability and homicide. A Review of the literature. Retrieved from https://ojp.gov. January 21, 2018

Hetherington, E.M. & Kelly, J. (2000). For Better for Worse: Divorced Discovered. New York. Norton 240-247

Hewlett, S.A. & Gonzales, T. (2013). Innovation, Diversity and Marketing Growth. Retrieved from https://coqual.org.org

High, M. (2015). "The reality of the American dream" Xavier Journal of Undergraduate Research: vol 3, Article 2. Available at https://www.exhibit.xavier.edu/xjournal/vol3/issu/2

Hospers, G.J. (2003). Creative cities, breeding places in the knowledge economy. Knowledge Technology and Policy, 16(3): 143-162

Howard, J. (2018) Gun death in U.S. reaches highest level in 40 years. Retrieved from https://www.cnn.com/2018/12/13/health/gun-deaths-highest-40-years-cdc/index.html

Ingram, G. (2019). What every American should know about foreign aid. Retrieved from https://booking.edu/policy2020vertical/what-every-american-should-know-abou-foreign-aid

Meatto, R. (2018). Still separated, still unequal: Teaching about school segregation and educational inequality. Retrieved from https://www.nytimes.com/2019/05/02/learning/lesson-plans/still-separate-still-unequal-teaching-about-school-segregation-and-educational-inequality.html

Minta, K. (2007). The reversed Diaspora – African Immigrants and the return home. University of Pennsylvania

Logan, J.R. (2015). Separate and unequal; The Neighborhood Gap for Blacks, Asians and Hispanics in metro America. Providence. R.I: Brown University.

Low, J. & Kevin, D. (1998) Structure and casual connection in children. On line television narratives. Cognitive Development. 13:201-225

Lin, J.C. (1997). Asian international student's adjustment issues and program suggestions. Journal of International Student 32, 473-479.

Kuo, Y.H. (2011). Language challenge faced by International graduates in the United States. Journal of International Students 1(2)38-42

Pal, J. (2014). What 126 studies tell us about education technology. Retrieved from www.News.met.edu/2014/met/what-126-studies-ell-us-about-education-technology

Patrick, L., & Kumar, V.R. (2012). Managing workplace diversity: Issues and challenges. https://sgo.sagepub.com

Petrie, G. (2004). Firearm and violence. A Critical Review. Washington DC ISBN 978-0-09

Propal, F. (2022). Housing for Immigrants. Immigrant Affairs Manager. City of San Diego

Rigg, K. (2019). School-Based Drug Prevention Programs. https://www.psychologytoday.com/us/blog/drugs-and-the-people-who-use-them/201909/school-based-drug-prevention-programs

Robinson, G. & Dechant, K. (1997) Building a business case for diversity. The Academy of Management Executives, 11(31), 21-31

Schwartz, J.F. (1995). Childhood Sociodemographic and Psychological Factors, as a Predictors of Mortality Across the Life Span. American Journal of Public Health: 1237-1245

Seltzer, A.J. & Bianchi, S.M. (1988)

Stewart, T. (2019). How can we prevent mass shooting.in the United States. Retrieved from

Shirak, A. (2016). Entrepreneurship starting a business Retrieved from https:/hacl.handle.net/1011972981 e

Walia, M.S. & Malik, E. (2015). Workforce diversity management: Essence of modern organization: Educational Board

Winthrop, J. "A model of Christian Charity" Hanover Historical Text Project. August 1996. (April 22, 2011) https://history.hanover.edu./whintrop.html

Woodrow, C.J. (2018). Scarred by school shooting. Washington Post. Retrieved: May 29, 2018

Wilson, D. & Daly, G. (1992). Who killed Whom in Spouse killing, Criminology? 30(2) 189-215

Wood, G. (2013). Why the declining marriage rate affects everyone. Retrieved from https://heritage.org/marriage/why-the-declining-marriage-rate-affects-everyone

U.S. Small Business Administration (2016). Is entrepreneurship Retrieved from

U.S. Small Business Administration (2016). Qualifying as a small business Retrieved from https://www.sba/gov/contracting/gov-standard-contracting-quality--smolall-business/

Volkow, N. (2017). Federal efforts to combat opioid drug abuse and addition crisis. Retrieved from drugabuse.gov/about.nida/legistlative-activities-towards-congress/

About the Author

Dr. Emei Ezidinma was born in Nigeria as the youngest of seven children, growing up in a vibrant and close-knit family. From a young age, he demonstrated a thirst for knowledge and a deep curiosity about the world beyond his hometown. It was his high school teacher, an American Peace Corps volunteer, who ignited Dr. Ezidinma's desire to migrate to the United States, exposing him to the limitless possibilities that awaited him across the ocean.

In his captivating book, "The Journey from Africa to Achieve the American Dream," Dr. Ezidinma shares his remarkable insights into the challenges and triumphs he encountered in his quest to actualize his dream. As an esteemed expert in leadership and management, he offers valuable information and guidance that sustains the courage and hope of dreamers who face their own obstacles.

Beyond his literary achievements, Dr. Ezidinma is a successful entrepreneur, having built thriving businesses in various industries. His drive and determination have not only propelled him to personal success but have also fueled his deep commitment to giving back to the community. He firmly believes in making the world a better place, and his philanthropic endeavors reflect his dedication to creating positive change.

With his wealth of knowledge and experience, Dr. Ezidinma has become a sought-after speaker, inspiring audiences with his remarkable journey and empowering them to pursue their dreams relentlessly. His engaging storytelling and profound insights captivate listeners, leaving a lasting impact on those fortunate enough to hear him speak.

As an immigrant who has lived in the United States for over four decades, Dr. Ezidinma's unique perspective offers a wealth of wisdom to readers seeking guidance on achieving success in America and beyond. His academic and professional accomplishments, coupled with his unwavering dedication to personal growth, make him an exceptional mentor for individuals from all walks of life.

"The Journey from Africa to Achieve the American Dream" is just the beginning of Dr. Ezidinma's mission to uplift and inspire. With his boundless passion, entrepreneurial spirit, and commitment to giving back, he continues to empower others to overcome obstacles and make their dreams a reality. Dr. Emei Ezidinma's story is a testament to the power of resilience, hard work, and faith—a story that encourages readers to embrace their own journeys and reach for the heights of their dreams.

www.ingramcontent.com/pod-product-compliance
Lightning Source LLC
Chambersburg PA
CBHW060917120626
46553CB00001B/358